Mytton of Halston

ISBN 9780955034336
Printed and bound in Great Britain.
Published by Nigel J Hinton 2021

Photographs and illustrations: Nigel J. Hinton, Poppy Hinton.

Acknowledgements

Thanks to Neil and the late Sibley Mytton, the first Myttons I met when I came to work in Shrewsbury in the 1970s. Neil was a design engineer and I was the financial director at the former Hartley Electromotive Ltd business, later renamed as Shrewsbury Technology Ltd. We shared an interest in golf and the history of Shrewsbury, Shropshire and Wales. Neil has given me access to his family archive.

Thanks to friends and family, especially Bridget Hinton, who assisted with the research and general advice. Thanks to Rupert and Harriet Harvey of Halston Hall, who gave permission for me to visit and take photographs of the Hall, the Estate and the Chapel. I am grateful to David Thornycroft, a descendent of General Mytton, who gave me access to his publication *In Direct Descent* which was an important and useful source of information.

The staff at Shropshire Archives, in Oswestry and Shrewsbury have been very supportive and giving guidance and assistance to me on my visits there. Maria Neergheen has proof read the drafts and given advice and helpful suggestions on the presentation of the book. I would also thank Dr James Bowen for advice and Giles Carey for arranging permission to quote from HER PRN 00871 – Halston

About the Author

Nigel J Hinton M.A. F.C.A FRHistS is a retired chartered accountant with a passion for local history, he and his wife Bridget are both qualified guides in Shrewsbury and their family is based in Shropshire. Nigel is a past master of the Shrewsbury Drapers Company and a trustee of VCH Shropshire. When time allows Nigel plays golf and the saxophone, but not at the same time.

Nigel's other publications include *Historical Hostelries* with David Trumper; *Silhouette, The Story of the Little X*, about Shrewsbury's famous corset and underwear factory; *Baa Baa Blodwyn* illustrated by Carol Davies; *The Shrewsbury Drapers' Company 1462-2017*; *Shrewsbury at Work* and *Wool War & Wealth*.

Preface

Myttons have been established in Shropshire for centuries and the name is recorded in the Domesday Book. They have provided the towns with mayors of Shrewsbury and Oswestry, the counties with high sheriffs of Shropshire and Merioneth and MP for Shrewsbury and Shropshire. The family built a property empire by hard work, marriage and later after the Reformation by exchange when Halston was acquired. This book briefly describes nineteen generations of Mytton, their families and their contribution to the history of Shrewsbury and Shropshire. The book goes some way to balance their reputation against the damage to it done by John Mad Jack Mytton.

Born in 1796 John Mytton became selfish, ruthless and drank heavily. He was known as Mad Jack Mytton for his exuberant horse riding and life style. The first biography was written by his friend Charles James Apperley, who wrote as Nimrod. He holds Jack as an example of how not to live a life and as a warning to others. Jack was a bully and very cruel to his wives. Totally irresponsible in terms of looking after money he made little provision for his family. He had a complete disregard for his own personal safety, whilst at the same time he endangered others and was responsible for the death of an innocent person. Although I started with some sympathy towards him after concluding research for this work any sympathy evaporated and I decided he may have been mad but he was a very Bad Jack Mytton.

Historic England have produced a detailed report on Halston Hall and the estate which I could not improve on so it is reproduced in full in the final section with permission. To conclude there are some notes of the Mytton legacy to be found around the county of Shropshire.

Contents

List of Illustrations

Introduction

The first section of this book examines the early foundations of the family of Mytton, and throws a light onto their achievements in the local counties and nationally and describes how they accumulated land and property in Shropshire and neighbouring counties. The next section will explore the life of John Mytton, his family, military career, relationships, character and legends. The final section will look in detail at the history of Halston, the Hall, the Chapel and the Estate.

The early spelling of the name was `de Mutton` and it also appears as Mitton, the form Mytton came into general use during the sixteenth century. Forenames also changed as in Reginold, which became Reginald. After this introduction this work will use the current spelling of forenames and Mytton thereafter.

Mytton is mentioned in the *Domesday Book, Shropshire*:[1]

> *Now in the parish of Fitz. It was in Baschurch Hundred (2) in 1086. It would seem that the 1086 tenant Picot (of say) alienated it from St. Mary`s of Shrewsbury and incorporated it in his manor of Fitz (4,20,15), since it soon ceased to be an independent manor; see Eyton x p. 156. Picot likewise appears to have alienated chinbaldescote from the Church of St Mary of Bromfirld (4,20,21 note). NOW IT IS AT A REVENUE FOR 11sDB Firma has several meanings, but here the phrase ad firman pro seems to mean that the manor was being held at a revenue, for a money rent, that it was being farmed.[2]*

Gelling includes Mitton c.1220-30. [3]Also included is Mutton 1255-6 *Ass et freq with variations in spelling to 1383. With* SBL 3770, *A collection of Shropshire documents held in the Local*

Studies Department of Shropshire Libraries in the Shropshire Archives. [4]

Although the name Mytton has a French origin, the earliest of the Thornycroft family legends tell of their lineage back to Sir Everard or Edward Mytton killed in 1154 during the wars of Stephen and Matilda.[5]

The legend continues with Edward`s son Alfred, followed by Sir Hugh, then Roger followed by Stephen, then Owen followed by Phillip to William and then to John.[6]

John de Mytton, a merchant, appears on the guild merchant roll of 1372.[7] He married Anne, the daughter of Sir Paul Dorrell and his wife Anne, who was daughter of Sir Roger Powis, Knight. John de Mutton and Anne had at least one son named Henry or Hankyn.

Hankyn Mytton (1335- ?), was married to Alicia. The pedigree of Mytton is proved and undoubted authenticity from Hankyn de Mytton downwards according to Blakeway who states *"The first undoubted progenitor of the Halston family is Hankyn Mitton, an abbreviation of Henry."*[8]

Mytton in the Fifteenth Century

Reginald Mytton MP d.1424

Reginald was the son of Hankyn and Alicia Mytton. He was astute in his personal life and acquired much wealth and property in and around Shrewsbury by his marriage settlement to Anna, the daughter of William Vaughan ii.[9] They had two sons Thomas and John.[10]

Reginald was MP in 1373 and bailiff of Shrewsbury in 1390. He gained enough wealth to be able to lend forty marks to Richard II, during one of his visits to Shrewsbury when the Parliament was held in the Abbey.[11]

As a leading and prosperous merchant some of his activities were too ambitious. He over-reached himself when he and a fellow exporter and wool trader, John Grafton were indicted in 1413 for defrauding their suppliers in Shropshire.[12]

William Vaughan (I) was a very successful wool merchant, included in the handful of `super-rich` merchants of Shrewsbury having joined the guild merchant, as a non-Shrewsbury resident, on the forinseci list, in 1268. By the following year he held six burgages within the borough and a part of another in Frankwell.[13] He founded the Vaughan dynasty and the fortune and by 1319 he had passed it to Thomas Vaughan who was described as the richest man in Shrewsbury.[14]

It appears that William Vaughan (II) had retained his inheritance and was able to gift substantial property in a marriage settlement to Reginald Mytton. This included Vaughan`s Mansion.

Vaughan's Mansion as it appeared in the 18th century.

1. Vaughan`s Mansion                     Author`s Collection
H E Forrest   *Old Houses of Shrewsbury*

Thomas Mytton (1410-)

Thomas was the surviving elder son of Reginald Mytton and
Eleanor le Skinner. Thomas increased the family wealth and
property portfolio by marrying Cecilia (Agnes).[15] She was
daughter and heir of William Burley, and also heir of the Pride
and the Tour families. Their only son Thomas was born in 1440,
the same year Thomas senior is listed bailiff in Dr Taylors MS.[16]

> *In the environs of Coton Hill there was a chapel and
> hermitage of St Catherine, first recorded in 1395 in the
> deed of an adjoining property.[17] It was the responsibility
> of the Pride family before 1408 but later passed to the*

Myttons. According to Baker it was still extant in 1521 at that year's borough rental.[18]

After the Great Fire in Shrewsbury in 1393,[19] which destroyed many buildings from St Julian's Church to the English Bridge, the aptly named Mytton's Mansion was rebuilt, at 66/67 Wyle Cop, in about 1430.[20]

Moran states that this is *`a similar range to Henry Tudor House though less elaborate with a smaller though well moulded and coved entrance passageway, which would admit a donkey train but not large carts. Jettied at two levels with exposed bull-nosed joints and another tallyman's window over the entry`.* [21]

2. Mytton's Mansion on Wyle Cop   Author's photograph

Thomas Mytton MP (1440 -1504)

Thomas Mytton was a surviving son of Thomas and Cecilia Burley. He was driven and ambitious and he further increased the Mytton wealth. He married Elinor, the daughter of Sir John Burgh, of Wattlesborough, Dinas Mawddwy, and Radbroke. They had a son William. Her family included Owen Glendower and Griffin ap Rhys, Prince of South Wales. The settlement included properties in Habberley and Dinas Mawddwy, not only was the income and status useful, but doors opened for his political advancement. Thomas is also recorded as marrying a daughter of Booth of Cheshire and their union produced Sir Adam Mytton.[22] Other sources state he married Anna a relative of Jeffrey Kyffyn.[23]

Thomas was elected bailiff 11 times between1464-1504,[24] and acquired the Marcher Lordship of Mawddwy.[25] He became MP for Shrewsbury in 1472.[26] Sheriff of Shropshire in 1483.[27]

A high point in his glittering career occurred in 1480, whilst he was high-sheriff of Shropshire; he captured the rebel Duke of Buckingham and was rewarded with a generous gift from Richard III, of Caus Castle, previously owned by Buckingham.[28]

> *Caus Caurs or Chaurs Castle sat on a ridge above the River Rea WNW of Pontesbury although now little remains of the castle the mound and elements of construction lines are still visible and the street plan of the borough of Cause could be traced until the early nineteenth century. Jackson suggests that the nearby Hawcocks Mount was founded by William Corbet around the time of the Conquest but was confiscated from his son Roger because he supported the rebellion of Roger de Belleme. But by 1176 it was back in the family and held*

*by Robert Corbet, and the rebuilding he commenced was
completed by his son Thomas. It then passed to the de
Leybourne family and in 1347 to the Staffords who were
created dukes of Buckingham. In 1645 it was captured by
Parliament forces and demolished and the local roads
were improved by using masonry from the castle, any
remaining stone work has largely been recycled.*[29]

Thomas Mytton became renowned for a well-known
exercise in diplomacy, when he had to face a dramatic dilemma
over his loyalty to Richard III, in 1485. There was a serious threat
to the security of Shrewsbury when an army headed by Henry
Tudor, Earl of Richmond, approached the town from Wales.
Thomas had said earlier that Henry Tudor would only enter the
town over his body. As the army approached closer Thomas gave
instructions for the gates to be locked to keep Henry Tudor out.

When Henry Tudor duly arrived, he could not gain
entrance, so he retired to regroup. But naturally he returned with
his army the next day in a more belligerent mood and was
determined to take Shrewsbury by force if necessary. The
dilemma was to save the town or remain loyal to Richard and
Thomas produced an elegant solution. He said that if the troops
promised to behave well and agreed not to ransack the town, he
would let them enter. He then lay down and Henry Tudor stepped
over him and honour was satisfied as Thomas kept his oath of
loyalty to Richard III.[30]

3. The Old Welsh Bridge   Author's Collection
H E Forrest   *Old Houses of Shrewsbury*

Thomas Mytton was one of the first to join the fraternity of St
Winifred founded on 9 February 1487, by Abbot Thomas Mynde
of St Peter's, the Abbey Church, when he was granted a Royal
license to found a perpetual fraternity in St Winifred's honour.[31]

Mytton in the Sixteenth Century

William Mytton MP (1465-1513)

Only son of Thomas Mytton's first marriage to Elinor Burley, he gained a half-brother, when his father married for the second time, a daughter of a man named Stanley, and they had a son they named Adam Mytton, born 1498. William later married Cicely, daughter of Sir Henry Delves of Doddington in Cheshire. They had a son Richard, in 1500. William relocated from Vaughan's Place to outside the town walls in Coton Hill.[32] He was sheriff of Shropshire in 1544.[33]

4. Former Great Barn on Coton Hill   Author's Photograph
Forrest suggests that the Mytton Mansion faced the River Severn.[34]

William had also inherited the marcher lordship of Mawddwy, which included the manor of that name and the ancient borough of Dinas Mawddwy. Held of the Lords Grey of Powis in socage. (A feudal way of holding land by the tenant performing specified services or by payment of rent, but not requiring military service). Although the value of ten marks a year was small, when William Mytton died in 1513, the marcher lordship was of a greater value than the monetary value implied.

William was an alderman and six times bailiff of Shrewsbury, Lord of Mawddwy, chief steward of the Manor of Church Stretton and known to all as "gentle master Mytton." Three times a bailiff, he was selected for parliament and became MP for Shrewsbury in 1491.[35] At his death William Mytton also possessed 200 houses in Habberley, Shrewsbury and elsewhere from his father. Included in the Shrewsbury lands was land in Monkmeole and Crowmeole held under a ninety-nine-year lease dated 21 April 1507 from the Abbey of Buildwas. The freehold of this land was acquired by purchase around the time of the Dissolution.[36]

Sir Adam Mytton MP (1498 -1561) [37]

Son of Thomas Mytton of Vaughan Place, and Coton Hill, Shrewsbury, by his second wife, this made him the half-brother of William Mytton and uncle of Richard Mytton.
He married Alice, daughter of one of the Bowdler family, the widow of Thomas Withyford`s second daughter Catherine.

Adam Mytton was active in local administration becoming a Burgess in Shrewsbury by 1520, he was appointed coroner 1521-2, auditor 1522-3, bailiff 1523-4, 1527-8, 1531-2, 1537-8, 1541-2, 1546-7, 1552-3. An alderman by 6 March 1525. He was elected as MP for Shrewsbury in 1523, 1529, 1536, and again in 1542. He was later knighted.

As a tax collector he was a commissioner for the subsidy roll in Shrewsbury in 1524. He spread his wings and became a chantries commissioner for Wales and Monmouth in 1546. Four years later he was appointed commissioner for relief, Shropshire, and Shrewsbury in 1550. In 1553, he was commissioner for goods of churches and fraternities in Shrewsbury and Radnorshire. Commissioner for Loans in Salop in 1557 and a justice in Salop and other adjacent counties.

He was a member of the Council of Wales and the Marches by 1543 until his death in 1561. High-sheriff of Radnorshire in 1546-7 and 1552-3, he was also appointed high-sheriff for Shropshire in 1553-4; recorder of Bridgnorth in 1550-until his death, and steward, Clun and Oswestry by 1561. Although he was a younger son Adam Mytton inherited his family's original home in Shrewsbury. He followed a traditional path to local eminence, the first step being during 1518-19, when he joined the Shrewsbury Drapers' Company. The Drapers controlled the Shropshire cloth trade and that control was beginning to be contested by the Mercers' Guild. He was appointed as a warden of the Shrewsbury Drapers' Company in 1520-1 and its steward in 1526-7.

Mytton defended an action brought by the Exchequer against the Drapers' Company, by asking the Queen to confirm their title to land, that brought in income that Commissioner Henry Knyvet claimed was used to maintain a priest.[38]

Once Mytton had established himself in the Shrewsbury Drapers' Company and in local administration, his membership of Parliament was the next obvious step in his progress. He was following in his father's footsteps and family precedent, as in 1437, his great-grandfather William Burley had been an MP and was selected as speaker of the House.

Adam Mytton's election to Parliament in 1523 almost certainly represented a victory for the Drapers` for both he and his partner Edmund Cole were members of that Company. He was presumably the Drapers' nominee in the two following Parliaments (and again in 1542), but on both of these occasions he sat with a mercer of noble origin, Robert Dudley, alias Sutton. Although these two men represented opposing factions, no ill feeling is known to have existed between them. When they were returned in the year 1529, they may have been already related by marriage and during the 1530s they were to be associated in local issues.

Adam Mytton did not sit for Shrewsbury in the Parliament of 1539, but three years later he made his fourth and final appearance in the House, sitting this time with his nephew Richard Mytton. No details have come to light of his part in the proceedings of the Commons, but when he petitioned Thomas Cromwell in 1538 for some former monastic property in Shrewsbury, he reminded the minister that for 16 or 17 years he had been *"one of the number of the members who at all times to my little power were ready to prefer the King's cause"*, and that during the Parliament of 1536, he had been advised by Cromwell, to spare no labour in soliciting anything in the King's gift in Shropshire, that he would like in reward.

He was not only an administrator, in 1536 he raised and commanded 100 men against the northern rebels. His exemplary loyalty and his association with Thomas Cromwell,[39] whose 'accepted' servant he considered himself, qualified him for a higher status in local administration than he had hitherto enjoyed, and in 1538 he was named for the first time to the Shropshire bench. The fall of Cromwell did not harm him, and by 1543 he had been appointed to the Council of the Marches of Wales, of which he remained an active member until his death. This appointment brought with it a considerable extension of influence and later, in 1547, a knighthood. During the late 1540s and 1550s these appointments called for much journeying throughout the Marches and in Wales.

Although his own parliamentary career ended in 1544, Adam Mytton used his various offices to obtain seats in the Commons for kinsmen, friends and clients of the council. He made a second home for himself in Radnorshire, but his absences from Shrewsbury did not diminish his prestige there, indeed he acted as the council's spokesman in the town. It is suggested by Davidson & Hawkyard that he arranged for John Evans to be elected to Parliament early in Edward VI's reign. He was flexible and he adapted to regime change in the Dissolution, as in 1546-7, when he supervised the public burning of religious paintings taken from local churches.

His alleged failure as sheriff to send the precept to New Radnor Boroughs for the election there, in the autumn of 1553, gave rise to acrimony and to an action against him in the Exchequer by the attorney-general. Mytton answered the charge in the Michaelmas term 1554, arguing that the case should be dismissed because statutes governing elections in England did not apply to Wales. The outcome is not recorded.

At the beginning of Mary's reign, Adam Mytton as a leading Protestant had managed to get a pardon covering his activities in Shrewsbury and Presteigne. He had given up his second house by 10 July 1561, when as a sick man he made his will. He left his wife all his property in Shrewsbury and its suburbs, then after remembering his servants he divided the remainder of the estate between his two daughters. He named his wife executrix, and his nephew Richard Mytton and his friend John Bradshaw overseers: the will was proved on the following 4 October 1461.[40]

Adam was involved with the commissions who reported to the Regency council of Edward VI on the details of the amount of plate remaining in Shrewsbury churches in 1552. Under suffrage of the bishop of Dover, three Friaries in Shrewsbury were inspected and inventories were taken of plate and anything of value was taken into custody. It is possibly for this service he was honoured with a knighthood.

Adam Mytton did not always have an iconoclastic career and indeed a major improvement in the town was started during the time he was bailiff in 1552/3.[41]
An adventurer approached the council with a plan to install a fresh water supply to Shrewsbury town centre *via a good conduit through pipes from a spring or well commonly called Broadwell. The town agreed to supply wooded pipes, lead and lime and stone and to dig the trenches for the pipes.* [42]

By the time it delivered the water supply Adam's nephew Richard had become bailiff. The conduit head was a collecting tank associated with 9 wells in the vicinity, and provided a source of water for the town of Shrewsbury from 1556, the present building probably completed by 1578. The water was piped from this site, known as Broadwell, to several points within the town. The system was established under licence to the Corporation, and was acquired by the Corporation in 1878. It remained in use until 1947. Some of the urban conduit heads associated with this system still survive (Betton Street, Porthill Road, St Michael's Street, Sundorne Road, Town Walls}.

5. Conduit Head   Author's Photograph

Small gabled structure comprising a single chamber accessed by
small inserted doorway in gable, with brick lined water tank
inside. Gables have cambered trusses with bracing and collar,
and are slatted. Moran states that it seems incredible that it dates
from 1578 but the documentary evidence for that year is clear.
Certainly, she added, its stone walls and remarkably heavy roof
trusses, which would not be out of place in a cathedral, are
testimony to the fact it was built to last.[43]

Richard Mytton MP (1500-1591) [44]

Grandson of Thomas Mytton, and nephew of Adam Mytton he
lived long and had three wives and sixteen children. Of these
three of his sons married being Edward, John and Thomas.[45]

John moved to Pontyscowrid in Montgomery and this line of the family became The Myttons` of Garth when his descendant Richard Mytton 1683 -1775, in 1717 married the only daughter and heiress of Brockwell Wynn of Garth, Gent.[46]

Of the children, (the number of which varies with sources) twelve of these came from his first marriage to Agnes Anne, daughter of Sir Edward Grey of Enville. His second wife was a daughter of Jenkyn Pigot of Rhuddlan. His third wife was Elinor an heiress, her father being Sir George Harborne, a lawyer and recorder of Shrewsbury, she was the widow of Richard Beeston of Shrewsbury. A pious woman she spent six hours each day on her knees at prayer. She outlived William and died aged ninety in January 1602.[47]

Richard was an alderman in Shrewsbury 1538, and bailiff 6 times in the years 1542-3, 1549-50, 1553-4, 1557-8, 1561-2, 1567-8. He was a justice of the peace in Shropshire 1543-54 and later in Merioneth in 1558/59. He was also high sheriff of Salop in 1543-4 and again in 1559-60, and high sheriff in Merioneth in 1546-7 and 1553-4. In 1550, he found time to be a commissioner of relief in Shrewsbury and Merioneth. He was well connected as a servant to earls of Arundel by 1547,[48] and also served as steward of the Oswestry lordship.[49]

It is recorded that in 1529 he was a member of the Inner Temple, where he had shared a chamber since 1525 but is not mentioned again. Nothing in his later career suggests that he acquired more knowledge of the law than was needed by a country gentleman.

It may have been due to his work at the Inner Temple that Mytton owed his entry to the House of Commons: in 1529 he was returned for Devizes, a borough with which he had no known personal tie. Devizes was then held in jointure by Catherine of Aragon, who spent time in Ludlow following her marriage to Prince Arthur before he died and prior to her marriage to Henry VIII. The patronage of the two boroughs was evidently exercised by her vice-chamberlain Sir Edward Darrell, himself one of the knights of the shire in this Parliament.

Later Richard Mytton was elected for local seats, Shropshire 1539, Shrewsbury 1542, Shropshire 1545, Shropshire March 1553, Shropshire October 1553, Shrewsbury 1554, Shropshire November 1554.

Mytton was well placed to take on leases of the former and now dissolved monastic properties that had been granted to Shrewsbury in a new charter in 1542.[50] As a lawyer of the Inner Temple he was wealthy enough and knew his way around the legislation. He was elected as bailiff for Shrewsbury in 1542, but he declined payment for this and only took part of his parliamentary wages, and it may be that this action reflects Mytton`s altruism

By that time Richard Mytton had done well out of the Dissolution, taking leases of a number of ex-monastic properties in Shropshire.[51] In April 1539, he was granted a five-year lease of the whole Halston estate except Kinnerley rectory and Dolgynwal, he was required to live at Halston, to provide hospitality, and to find a priest for the chapel.

In 1543 the Halston demesne was granted by the Crown to John Sewster and it was excluded from a new lease made to Mytton in 1545. Sewster, however, sold Halston in 1544 to Alan Horde, who later exchanged it for lands in Warwickshire owned by Mytton in 1551.[52] Thus Halston became home to this branch of Mytton family until it was sold in 1847.

In 1545 Richard stood surety for a payment due from the twelfth Earl of Arundel to the crown.

The marriage between John Fitz Alan (1223 - 1267) and Isabel, one of the co-heirs of Hugh d'Aubigny, earl of Arundel, brought the honour of Arundel and the title of earl to the Fitz Alan family in 1243.[53]

Later the earl was to be instrumental in obtaining for him, with the help of the Duke of Somerset, leases of tithes in Shropshire and of St. Mary's College, Shrewsbury. Mytton was involved in a number of Star Chamber cases, some over property and one over a disputed jurisdiction in a liberty, probably the Earl of Arundel's; none of the decisions in these cases is extant. In May 1549 he had licence to purchase the manors of Osleston in Derbyshire and Sandford in Shropshire, from Sir Robert Curzon, another MP, who had built a property portfolio after the Dissolution.

Mytton was appointed to raise troops in Merioneth for the French war of 1544, in which Arundel distinguished himself at the taking of Boulogne, but as he was sheriff Mytton probably did not serve overseas. In 1548 Shrewsbury paid him 23*d* at his departure with the armed men to the Earl of Arundel, an operation which may have been connected either with a muster of troops in the county or with the despatch of reinforcements to the Scottish border.

Mytton was well placed to be elected knight of the shire, an MP,[54] for the second time. He was not elected to the Parliament of 1547, but was returned in March 1553.

Mytton was involved with the capture of one of the rebel leaders, Lord Thomas Grey, near Oswestry in February 1554, and his delivery to London for eventual execution. This left Mytton open to much litigation between 1554 and 1562, when he had to defend actions in Chancery, King's bench. These all related to the money and goods in Grey's possession at the time of his capture. The bulk of these, including a claim for £200 in cash and two jewelled rings, were brought by the plaintiff, Elizabeth Dannett, claimed by grant from the Queen. Among Mytton's alternative lines of defence was one denying the Queen's right to dispose of the goods of traitors and felons captured at Oswestry, 'being a town of liberty of the right honourable Henry Earl of Arundel', and asserting his own, as the earl's officer there. The outcome is unknown.[55]

But Mytton disappeared from public life and Parliament but remained active in Shrewsbury. It is suggested by the Parliamentary historian D F Coros this was the price he paid for his religious conservatism. Mytton continued to depend upon the dissident Arundel. Having sat in the first three Marian Parliaments.[56]

Mytton sued out a pardon on the accession of Elizabeth, when he was described as a resident of Shrewsbury. He presumably devoted the rest of his long life to the management of the family estates; part of these he is known to have transferred in his lifetime, to his son Edward who pre-deceased him in 1568.

In 1580, when he must have been aged about 80 years old, Richard appeared on the Muster Roll as one of the 126 members, and their servants, of the Shrewsbury Drapers` Company.

> *Richard Mitton esquire, in armor.* Later he is included in the roll of 1587 as *Richard Mytton, esquire, in Armor, a Corslett with a bill, sword, & dager. His servants Thomas Clemson, John Hugh Davies William ap Roland.*[57]

He survived nearly all his sons and at least one grandson and he died intestate on 26 November 1591, aged 90.

Mytton was buried in St. Chad's Church, Shrewsbury, where a monument commemorated him. An anonymous Shrewsbury chronicler also recorded the passing of "the gentle Master Mytton" and later celebrated the virtues of his last wife, who survived him, dying on 30 January 1602 also at the age of 90.[58]

6. Old St Chad`s Church        Author`s Collection
H E Forrest Old St Chads   *Old Churches of Shrewsbury*

7. Halston Hall   Author`s Collection
Cathrall William, *History of Oswestry* (Oswestry 1871)

Edward Mytton (I) (1520-1568)

The son of Richard Mytton MP (1500-1591) by his first wife
Agnes Anne, elder daughter of Sir Edward Grey of Enville.
Edward lived in Habberley and later Halston. In 1552 he married
Anne the daughter of Sir Edward Greville of Milcote
Warwickshire. They had seven children Edward (II), Richard,
Lewis also known as Ludovick, Elinor, Cassandra, Margaret and
Jane.

      He was elected to the Corporation of Shrewsbury in 1561.
Later in 1564 he was arrested by order of the Privy Council and
sent to The Fleet Prison by the Bishop of London for hearing
Mass. He was pardoned before coming to trial in 1566, and died
two years later.[59] He predeceased his father Richard by twenty-
three years.

Thomas Mytton MP (1530-1563)

A son of Richard Mytton MP (1500-1591) and Agnes Anne elder daughter of Sir Edward Grey of Enville. He married Margaret, one of the seven daughters of Sir Edward Greville MP (c.1566 – 1634) of Milcote, in Warwickshire.

He was elected as MP in November 1554, without much experience as senior Member for Shrewsbury. He was helped by his father`s connections, who had held the seat in the previous Parliament and on this occasion as a knight of the shire.

Thomas Mytton was not one of those informed against in the King's bench during Easter term 1555 for leaving the Parliament before its dissolution without a licence. His attitude towards his arrears of 66 days attendance and travel expenses may have been influenced by his father's difficulties about that time, he did not sit in Parliament again. In 1560, Mytton was made escheator [60] for Merioneth and a year later appointed to the county bench, on which his father had previously served. He was renamed to the bench in 1562, and he is mentioned as bailiff of Wroxeter in 1563.[61] He also predeceased his father by twenty-eight years.

8. Halston Hall   Author`s Photograph

Edward Mytton (II) (1553-1583)

Son of Edward (I) and Anne the daughter of Sir Edward Greville
of Milcote, Warwickshire. Edward Mytton of Halston, was born
in 1553, succeeded as a minor in 1568 and died in 1583. He
married Anne in 1577 the daughter of Sir Reginald Corbet, Bart.
of Stoke, Judge of the Queen`s Bench, Chief Justice of North
Wales.[62] They had Richard (I) who entered Shrewsbury School
24 April 1593; Reginald entered Shrewsbury School 24 April
1593; fees were 3*s/*4*d* for Richard and 2*s/*6*d* for Reginald. Other
children were Peter of London; Edward; Elizabeth [63] He was only
thirty when he died and predeceased his grandfather.

Mytton in the Seventeenth Century

Richard Mytton (I) (1578 – 1640)

Son of Edward (II) and Anne the daughter of Sir Reginald
Corbet, Bart. and widow of Sir William Leighton of Plash. He
married Margaret Owen the daughter of Judge Sir Thomas Owen
of Condover Hall, who bought the estate in 1596 and the Hall
was almost completed before his death in 1598. Richard was
admitted to Lincolns Inn aged 16 by special request of his future
father-in-law.

9. Shrewsbury School   Author`s Collection

Peter Mytton (1582-1651)

A son of Edward (II) and Anne, he married Mary the daughter of
Rowland Lee. They had Edward of Park Lane, London, Peter
Thomas and Anne.

Peter had gone to London to seek his fortune in foreign trade. He joined the Merchant Taylors Guild and traded in Welsh Cloth using his Shropshire connections, his mother was linked to the families of Leighton and Corbett.[64] Mendenhall comments on the social status of gentry who entered trade using Peter Mytton as an example. He was involved in a case where London traders were buying and exporting wool direct from Wales, this was contrary to Drapers` ordinances of 1612. In 1634 he was listed as one of the leading shippers of Welsh cottons.[65]

General Thomas Mytton (1597 – 1656)

10. General Thomas Mytton 1596/7-1656   Author`s Collection
A drawing by Poppy Hinton

The son of Richard Mytton (I) of Halston, Shropshire, and his wife Margaret Owen, daughter of Thomas Owen of Condover. Thomas attended Shrewsbury School and he was prepared for university by a tutor James Wilding, the rector of Selattyn.[66] He matriculated at Balliol College, Oxford, on 11 May 1615, aged 18, and he became a pupil of chambers in Lincoln's Inn in the following year.

In 1629 Thomas Mytton married Margaret (or Magdalen) Napier (1605-1648) a daughter of Sir Robert Napier, 1st Baronet, of Luton Hoo in Bedfordshire (1560-1637). She was a sister of the second wife of General Sir Thomas Myddelton of Chirk, his fellow parliamentarian commander during the Civil War, a rare connection to the parliamentary party in the heavily royalist county of Shropshire. After Margaret`s death in 1649 he married Barbara Leonard, a daughter of Baron Dacre, there were no issue.

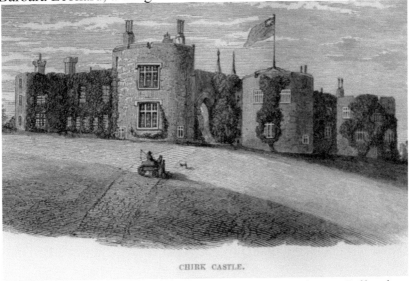

CHIRK CASTLE.

11. Chirk Castle   Author`s Collection
Cathrall William, *History of Oswestry* (Oswestry 1871)

Thomas and Margaret had at least seven children including: Richard (II), Edward and Mary, who became the wife of the royalist Sir Thomas Harris of Boreatton, when they were both aged 17. Another of their daughters Margaret 1624-1654 married Colonel Roger Pope, a parliamentarian. Sarah 1638-1698 married the Royalist Colonel and MP Sir Edward Acton, 1st Baronet. Magdalen married John Mytton of Melton Mowbray; Christian married Edward Raynesborough, a Colonel in the Parliamentary Army. This illustrates the issue for families in the English Civil War, who were split in their support for the opposing sides. [67]

Parliament had been challenging the prerogative powers of King Charles from late 1640 to 1642 when on 22 August 1642, the royal standard was raised in Nottingham, and this was seen as a formal declaration of war by King Charles against Parliament. The Parliamentary Army led by the Earl of Essex advanced into Northamptonshire and then Charles decided to move his smaller forces west to gather troops and funds in Shropshire. He arrived in Wellington on 19 September 1642. Here the King greeted his troops and local supporters then set out his objectives for the War against Parliament. He subsequently headed to Shrewsbury where his local supporters included Francis Ottley of Pitchford, who in addition to raising troops, had prepared his sovereign's way.[68]

At the Gay Meadow in Shrewsbury the King addressed the loyal Shropshire gentry.[69] Charles was hosted at The Council House where he stayed for three weeks,[70] whilst the loyalists gathered troops and money. Thus, he was in a much stronger position to fight the first battle of the Civil Way at Edge Hill on 23 October 1642.

Shrewsbury remained loyal to the crown until its capture in February 1645 by a small group from the garrison at Wem led by Captain John Benbow. There was support for Parliament's cause from many merchants, traders and Puritans, who were against the King mainly on religious grounds.[71] No major battles were fought in Shropshire during the conflict, and as Worton observes, Shropshire largely disappeared from the general histories of the Civil War.[72]

However, there were several local and bloody actions fought in Shropshire in which Thomas Mytton played a major part in the organisation and planning of the Parliamentary campaign. He was a member, and eventual leader of the local committee, set up by Parliament. Later in Worcester on 8 October 1642, Mytton was one of seventeen Parliamentarian activists from Shropshire, Worcestershire, Herefordshire and Gloucestershire who signed a declaration of mutual support.[73]

Six months later on 10 April 1643 the Parliament associated Shropshire with Warwickshire and Staffordshire under the command of Basil Feilding, 2nd Earl of Denbigh, Mytton remained as one of the Committee for Shropshire.

This led to the establishment of a Shropshire force by Sir William Brereton, who lobbied Parliament for support when his forces in Cheshire came under pressure.[74] According to Worton in his book *To Settle the Crown*, Thomas Mytton enjoyed an excellent reputation amongst local gentlemen including one who seeking a commission from Mytton said "Sir, I am resolved to do you service or no man".

On 11 September 1643 Sir Thomas Myddelton[75] and Mytton and their combined forces seized Wem, and here they established the first parliamentary garrison in Shropshire. Mytton was made governor, and in October fought off Lord Capel's attempt to recapture the town.

Mytton`s victory at Wem was inspirational and his popularity soared. Prior to this victory when the outcome was in doubt there were few volunteers for the Parliamentarian side. Later the commanders were able to report they could find 1,000 recruits, all of whom needed to be supplied with arms.

On 12 January 1644, Mytton and his troops surprised the cavaliers at Ellesmere, capturing Sir Nicholas Byron, Sir Richard Willis, and a convoy of ammunition. The Royalist response was to appoint Prince Rupert as head of the Royalist forces in the area.[76]

Not every action Mytton led was successful and he was defeated in an engagement near Longford in 1644, when Sir William Vaughan took Apley Castle. Mytton got his revenge in the following year winning a battle against Vaughan in 1645, near Denbigh in North Wales.[77]

In May 1644 the Earl of Denbigh and his army of about 2,500 marched into Staffordshire. They were responding to the advance of the King into Worcester and fought a successful defensive action at Tipton Green near Dudley where Mytton held a command.[78] The Earl of Denbigh resupplied Wem and then on 23 June, he joined with Mytton`s forces and together they captured the town of Oswestry.[79]

12. Oswestry Castle   Author`s Collection

Cathrall William, *History of Oswestry* (Oswestry 1871)

After taking Oswestry Colonel Mytton was appointed Governor on 23 June 1644, Lord Denbigh was ordered by the Committee of both Kingdoms, to go to Knutsford for a meeting with the other commanders in the region. They included Sir Thomas Middleton, commander of the North Wales forces, Sir William Brereton for Cheshire, Sir John Meldrum for Lancashire, Sir John Gell for Derbyshire and Lord Grey of Groby for Leicestershire. They were to join forces and stop Prince Rupert`s return before he could attack Sir William Waller in Gloucestershire.[80]

In the same year Colonel Mytton led a raid on the garrison at Atcham Bridge. His mounted troops rode around Shrewsbury travelling through Montford Bridge and Meole Brace disturbing animals and horses before withdrawing in the face of superior numbers of Royalist troops.[81]

In July 1644 Sir Thomas Myddleton was granted a licence, by the Committee of both Kingdoms, to start a campaign into Wales, as long as he continued his support for forces in Shropshire.[82] On 4 August Myddleton and Mytton led a small force of 550 horse, foot and dragoons from Oswestry joining up with two companies from Nantwich in Cheshire. Together they made a successful raid into Welshpool where Prince Rupert's Regiment of Horse were based. The brothers-in-law teamed up later to make a successful raid against Royalist forces in Ruthin in October.[83]

Later Mytton began to become estranged from the County committee of Wem, who were appointing and promoting their own officers without Mytton's approval.[84]

A problem for both the Parliamentarian and the Royalist armies, was that of securing and feeding prisoners, it was partly resolved, in July 1644, by a formal prisoner exchange. Mytton as governor of Wem made an agreement with the governor of Shrewsbury, Sir Fulke Hunkes, and one hundred prisoners were exchanged, with much drum banging, on the agreed day.[85]

On 1 August 1644 Mytton led a party of horse to interrupt supplies to Royalist forces by scattering cattle and sheep away from the Lamas Day harvest fair in Shrewsbury, thus depriving the opposition with much needed provisions.[86] Another raid into Welshpool caught Mytton's enemy by surprise and troops were scattered, but equally importantly, over two hundred horses were captured.[87]

On 22 February 1645 Mytton took part in the capture of Shrewsbury, though the credit was disputed between Mytton and Lieutenant-Colonel Reinking. The week before this successful raid an attack on Shrewsbury had failed due to it being a dark and wet night.[88] Led by a `forlorn hope` of 30-40 selected soldiers armed with swords, pistols and carbines with a similar number of musketeers armed with firelocks, which did not need smouldering match cord,[89] the small raiding party were able to take the castle as the main garrison troops were away on exercise.

Mytton took over the post as commander-in-chief of the forces of the six counties of North Wales on 12 May 1645 from his brother-in-law, Sir Thomas Myddelton. This followed the passing of the self-denying ordinance which led Myddleton, as a sitting member of parliament, being required to resign from his commission. Mytton was appointed High Sheriff of Shropshire on 30 September 1645. From this point he is frequently described as Major-General Mytton.

He took part in the defeat of Sir William Vaughan near Denbigh on 1 November 1645, frustrating the royalist`s attempts to relieve Chester and getting revenge for his defeat at Apley. A stand-off occurred in February 1646 when Mytton`s troops from Oswestry clashed with troops from Shrewsbury with both troops trying to collect assessments from the town of Ellesmere.[90]

Once Chester had fallen, Mytton went on to besiege the rest of the royalist garrisons in North Wales which in turn surrendered to Mytton`s forces: Ruthin (12 April 1646), Carnarvon (5 June 1646), Beaumaris (14 June 1646), Conwy Castle and town (9 August, 18 November 1646), Denbigh (26 October 1646), Holt Castle (13 January 1647), and Harlech Castle (15 March 1647).

Parliament maintained Mytton as commander-in-chief in North Wales. When the army was disbanded on 8 April 1647, he was appointed vice-admiral of North Wales. He was also granted £5,000 out of the estates of royalist delinquents.

In the Second Civil War, Mytton was again active on the Parliamentary side, and recovered Anglesey from the Royalists. Mytton did not shake his adherence to the Parliament, when in September 1651, he agreed to act as a member of the court-martial which sentenced James Stanley, 7th Earl of Derby to death.

Mytton represented Shropshire in the first Protectorate Parliament convened by Oliver Cromwell in 1654.

Thomas Mytton of Halston, above all others, was instrumental in keeping together the friends of the Parliament in the county of Shropshire, and in neutralizing in a great measure the influence of the Royalists there. And his superlative ability as a military commander, his unswerving fidelity to the Parliament, and his eminent humanity to his enemies, placed him in a more favourable light than any man in Wales, or the borders, who took sword in hand during that terrible struggle. [91]

General Thomas Mytton died in London in 1656, aged about fifty-nine, and was buried on 29 November in the Old St Chad's Church, Shrewsbury.

The will of Thomas Mytton 1656
Proved in London 4 November 1656, by Magdalen Mytton, power reserved to the other executors.
To my three daughters Magdalen, Christian and Sarah, £1,500 each for their portions, which is to be raised out of my lands and rents within several counties of Salop, Merioneth, Middlesex, Gloucester, Devon, Flint, Carnarvon, Anglesea and elsewhere. To my wife Lady Barbara Stapleton all her jewels and one piece of gold

which she now has worth £4, and all the furniture in the chamber where she now lodges, excepting my black cabinet and one steel spanner one gilt set of arms and one 22s piece of gold which same thing I bequest to my son Richard Mytton (underage). To my daughter my wrought purple bed. To my grandchild Thomas Pope £100 per year from my fee farm rents, which I have purchased in Anglesea. To my brother Sir Richard Napier best grey stone horse. To my friend Master Thomas Edwards of Kelelendray my watch with alarm. To my servant, John Booth, £5 yearly to be paid out of lands in Houghton. Executors; my kinsman Roger Kynaston of Hordley, Esq. Wm Jones of Sandford, Esq, and daughter Magdalen Mytton.

Henry Mytton MP (About1600 - after1651)

Henry Mytton MP of Melton Mowbray, Leicestershire and Westminster, was the grandson of Edward Mytton (I) of Halston, Henry married Frances, in November 1624 the daughter of Sir William Mynne of Epsom, Surrey. Henry became a Freeman of Much Wenlock in 1623-4 and was also elected as MP.

Healey, the parliamentary historian suggests that Mytton was probably raised in Leicestershire by his mother's family. However, there is nothing recorded before 1612, when his relative Sir Edward Greville granted him some lands at Sysonby, near Melton Mowbray. Although Greville's funds were limited and falling he maintained contacts at Court, which may have opened the door for Mytton to take a position of groom in the Privy Chamber in 1618. Within five years Mytton was promoted from groom to gentleman.

In 1624 he was elected as MP for Much Wenlock and he married Frances the sister of a gentleman pensioner, John Mynne from Leicester where he moved to. It seemed his new wife had good prospects, as her father, Sir William Mynne had left her a dowry of £1,000 and her brother-in-law George, Lord Berkeley, leased his lands to Mytton in Melton Mowbray.

Mytton became guardian of the minor daughter of Sir Edward Lawley, whose family had dominated Wenlock for three generations. He took his ward with him to Leicester and the move upset both her grandmother and the Wenlock Corporation. Later, he found a husband for his ward and she married Sir Roger Bertie. This move to another county did not go down well with the Wenlock voters as in the following election of 1626 Sir Thomas Lawley MP, First Baronet of Spoonhill, near Much Wenlock was returned unopposed.[92] The history is complicated as in the same period Henry Mytton of Shipton became bailiff of Wenlock liberty in 1622/3.

John Mynne's financial problems probably influenced his willingness to give permission for his sister to marry a man with few assets. John`s father, Sir William`s debts exceeded £6,000, John had to sell his patrimony and could not or would not pay his sister's portion, claiming that his entailed estates were not liable for the debt, and it is likely Mytton accepted a much lower sum.

It did not get any better when in 1634, Mytton lost his farm which may have been one of his only holdings of freehold land, when he ran into problems with the High Commission. By 1638 his debts totalled £1,100, and he was forced to ask for help from his sister-in-law Lady Berkeley who rescued him from his Leicestershire creditors.

Although he was a courtier, Parliament did not bring composition proceedings against his Leicestershire properties.

This suggested to Ferris, the parliamentary historian, that Mytton did not go to Oxford to join the King. But much of his income had ceased as the King did not pay him the usual Court fees and board allowances. During the Civil War his lands were fought over and he defaulted on interest payments to Lady Berkley. His last mention in history is in a Chancery suit in 1651.[93]

Richard Mytton (II) (1638-1670)

The son of General Thomas Mytton (1596-1656). He inherited Halston in 1656, as a minor and married Rebecca Kynaston daughter of Roger Kynaston of Hordley in 1658.
How he managed to retain Halston after the Restoration is uncertain. It has been suggested by Thornycroft family tradition that Richard was too young to participate in the Civil War, however after the Restoration he became a Royalist supporter and thus he hung on to the family seat.[94] Of their sons Richard being the eldest inherited Halston at the age of 10 as a minor; Edward (1660-1688) and Charles (1664-1711) emigrated to America. Daughter Mary was born in 1659 and another daughter, Sarah, married Edward Acton of Acton Scott.[95]

Richard Mytton MP (III) (1660-1718) [96]

He was the son of Richard Mytton (II) (1638-1670). Baptised on 27 December 1660, and educated at Shrewsbury School and Magdalen College, Oxford University in 1677. He joined the Inner Temple in 1679.
On 2 June 1685 he married Arabella Sarah, daughter of Sir John Houblon of St Christopher's, London, he became Lord Mayor in 1695, They had 8 sons and 7 daughters including Richard (IV) 1688; John (I) 1690; Edward 1691; William of Habberley 1693; James 1697; Henry 1700; Charles 1702, and Benjamin in 1705. Charles married Elizabeth Pigot in

about 1733. Their son Charles born in 1744 and his descendants took the name of Thorneycroft.

Their daughters were Mary (1686-1712); Anne (1687-1712); Arabella born 1689; Rebecca 1697; Sara 1699; Dorothy 1703; Esther 1707.

Richard (III) became a Freeman of Much Wenlock in 1684, then high sheriff of Salop in 1685–6. He was elected as MP for Shrewsbury in 1690-95, 1698-1709 and 1710-13.[97] He was an honorary member of the Mercers Company of Shrewsbury and twice sheriff of Merionethshire. Of their sons John (I) succeeded his brother Richard (IV).[98] Of their daughters, two died in infancy, four died unmarried and only one married, Arabella. Her husband was a Flintshire Squire named David Pennant. and Their son was Thomas Pennant the naturalist and traveller 1726-1798.

Under Richard`s supervision Halston Hall was rebuilt in about 1690, on an area of higher ground, as the location of the previous Hall near the Chapel was subject to flooding.

Although Richard had married into a family of rich Whig merchants; he was returned in 1690 as a Tory, and was classed as such in a list by Lord Carmarthen (Sir Thomas Osborne). It appears that he was not keen on Parliament and has been described as an inactive member, and Mytton was frequently absent. Protocol required a polite request to be away, but on 16 January 1692 a motion that he be granted leave of absence was rejected by the House, two days later he was given leave for a month. He took further two weeks leave on 6 February 1693, for health reasons and again on 15 December 1693, for three weeks and on 22 February 1695, again for three weeks.

At the next election he made way for his cousin John Kynaston, but was returned again in 1698 when the other outgoing Member for Shrewsbury, Hon Andrew Newport, also a

Tory, declined to stand. On 25 March 1699 he was granted three weeks leave of absence.

In the 1702 election Mytton and John Kynaston were for once faced with a contest at Shrewsbury, but they both easily defeated two Whigs. In this session, Mytton managed a private estate bill through the House and was given leave of absence for three weeks on 22 November. (See previous pages, Thomas Mytton MP 1530-1563.)

Mytton twice figured as a Tory in lists from 1708, in the election of that year he and Kynaston again repulsed a Whig challenge at Shrewsbury, only to be unseated on petition on 20 December 1709, the Commons endorsing a decision of the committee of elections which even Whig observers admitted had been grounded in little more than party prejudice.

In July 1710 he was one of a number of the Tory gentlemen and prospective parliamentary candidates who welcomed Dr Sacheverall to Shrewsbury at the head of a cavalcade of some 5,000 supporters. The popular and controversial preacher led the Tories to victory in the election of that year. Mytton topped the poll. In 1713 Mytton did not stand for re-election. He died in London on 22 October 1718 and was buried in Shrewsbury.[99]

Richard Mytton (IV) (1688-1730)

The son of Richard Mytton (III) (1660-1718) and Arabella Houblon. Richard (IV) married, Letitia, daughter of Roger Owen and heir to her brother of Condover in1719.[100]

Richard (IV) inherited Halston when his father died in 1718 and in 1730 it passed to his surviving brother John Mytton (I) (1690-1756). His daughter Anna Maria Mytton (1727- 1750) married Sir Charles Leighton Bart of Loton and London.[101] His other daughter Letitia (1729-1739) did not survive.

Mytton in the Eighteenth Century

John Mytton (l) (1690-1756)

The second son of Richard Mytton (1660-1718) and Arabella Houblon married Mary Elizabeth the daughter of Henry Davenport. They had Richard (1734-1736); John Mytton (II); (1737-1782); Barbara Letitia (1732- 1796); Sarah (1735-1806); Arabella (1737-1769).

He inherited Halston in 1730, when his elder brother Richard (IV) died. He was Mayor of Oswestry in 1732 and two years later, in 1734, he fought an election for Parliament against Sir Richard Corbet but lost.[102]

The Reverend William Mytton, (1693-1746)

A son of Richard (III) and Arabella Mytton. He was educated at Wadham College, Oxford, BA in 1714/15 and MA in 1719. He was incorporated at Cambridge in 1726. Rector of Habberley, an antiquary and a Shropshire genealogist. He died on 3 September 1746.[103]

A collection of his personal papers is contained in seven volumes held in The University of Birmingham, Cadbury Research Library. They include - Folio volumes of drawings, copies of manuscripts, pedigrees and transcriptions of inscriptions on gravestones and memorial tablets, made by and for William Mytton of Halston, Shropshire, relating principally to Shropshire churches. Copies are available in the Shropshire Archives. The drawings include sketches of funerary monuments, memorials and coats of arms, including representations of these in church windows. There are a small number of drawings of external views of churches and a limited amount of material relating to Shropshire historic monuments.

The collection includes much unpublished material relating to Shropshire. Cathrall quotes the late Rev C A Lloyd "Mr W Mytton was engaged for many years in collecting materials for a history of the County, but unfortunately died before he was able to arrange them."[104]

13. The Rectory, Habberley   Author`s Photograph

The Society of Antiquaries hold another collection of drawings of sepulchral monuments, arms, etc, in Shropshire, made for the Rev William Mytton shortly after his return from Italy in 1733. It was part of his collections for a history of Shropshire, by James Bowen, herald painter, of Shrewsbury; quoted from the account of books, etc, relating to Shropshire, appended to T F Dukes, Antiquities of Shropshire (1844). Many of the drawings are dated 1734. They consist of drawings (pen, wash, w/col), and arms in colour or trick, laid down. The collection includes churches and domestic buildings, monuments, incised slabs, brasses, arms from monuments and stained glass (ecclesiastical and secular). The arrangement is basically alphabetical, by parishes. Some of the arms in trick are copied from visitations at the College of Arms.[105]

14. St Mary`s Church, Habberley              Author`s Photograph

John Mytton (II) (1737-1782)

The second son of John Mytton (I) (1690-1756) he succeeded as his elder brother had already died aged 2 in 1736. He married Rebecca Pigot of Chetwynd in about 1767.[106] Another authority states he married the daughter of Robert Corbet. Their first son was John Mytton (III) (1768-1798) Their first daughter Rebecca (1769- 1770) did not survive so another daughter was given the same name Rebecca (1770- 1840) their last child another daughter was Maria (1773-1773), did not survive. John Mytton (II) became Mayor of Oswestry in 1771.

John (II) began some significant changes to Halston and these works were part of a general programme of improvements throughout the estate and were underway by the early 1770s. In 1776 he employed Robert Mylne to improve the Hall. The façade was altered and other work done on both the interior and exterior of the main building. These works may have been inspired by his experiences in Europe as they followed his return from the Grand Tour.[107] At considerable expense and trouble John (II) organised the draining of vast tracts of the low-lying ground which was greatly beneficial to the estate.[108] The Halston Estate Book, described as *A survey of the current state of the estate and proposals for its development* is in the handwriting of the late John Mytton (II). It has been heavily conserved and there are tantalising gaps in the majority of pages, however there is an index at the back.[109]

John Mytton (III) (1768- 1798)

The son of John Mytton (II) (1737-1782) and Rebecca Pigot of Chetwynd. He succeeded to Halston in 1782 aged fourteen. In 1793 he married Harriet Owen, daughter of William Mostyn Owen of Woodhouse. He became Mayor of Oswestry in 1792. On 30 September 1796 his first and only son John (IV) was born a seven-month child.[110] Christened 3 October 1796, the Rev William Davies officiated as chaplain. A daughter followed Harriet Rebecca (1798- 1826).

In 1794 it was a time of war and Parliament passed an Act authorising the raising of a corps of volunteers for the general defence of the country for the duration of the war and set out regulations for discipline and rates of pay.[111] In 1796 a further Act empowered the King to raise in each County a body of mounted men called `Provisional Cavalry`. This also carried the proviso that any person assessed for ten horses, kept for riding or driving, should be obliged to furnish one man and horse, completely equipped with horse furniture and uniform, according to a pattern supplied by the Government. Other persons keeping a lesser number of horses were to be divided into groups, according to the number of horses kept, and then a choice was made by ballot so that one horse was supplied for every ten horses in the group. There were penalties for absence from exercise or for failing to maintain equipment.

An oath of allegiance was required and service was limited to the duration of the war and one calendar month.[112]

In November in a letter to the Lord Lieutenant of Shropshire the Duke of Portland recommended a pattern of uniform to be adopted by the different Corps of Provincial Cavalry. The recommendations were a green jacket faced with scarlet and corded white, price 19s, green cloth pantaloons, 10s, leather cap and feather, 2s 6d, half boots,18s.[113] In the following year and in response to the threat of invasion by France the `Executive French Directory` issued a decree that "An Army shall be immediately assembled on the Sea Coast which shall be called the Army of England." In December a Bill was presented by Mr Pitt and passed for "Augmenting the Assessed Taxes by voluntary contributions to meet the present exigencies of the Public Service". King George III gave £200,000, matched by the Bank of England and in Shrewsbury, at a meeting on 19 February 1798, the Mayor of Shrewsbury and chairman Joseph Loxdale resolved to contribute £500 and then £200 per annum for the continuance of the war. Other contributions were made by individuals such as Sir William Pulteney, MP £5,000, and Sir Richard Hill, of Hawkstone, who contributed £1,200. These together with public collections from estate labourers, school boys and house servants were collected and a total of over £15,000 was raised in Shropshire for the national defences.[114]

In 1797 the Oswestry Rangers were raised by John Mytton Esquire. The officer`s commissions date from 6 April

1797 and the War Office list for 6 April 1797 show that the officers were Captain J Mytton; Lieutenant R Lloyd; Cornet L Venables and Adjutant G H Warrington.[115] The uniform was described as scarlet jacket, faced with green, helmets, sabres, and pistols. The troop was inspected on 7 July by Col Williams, when they mustered over 70 men and after inspection they dined together at the Guildhall. A Standard was presented to the Troop by Mrs Mytton. The ceremony was held in front of the Guildhall in the Square. The Standard was consecrated by the chaplain The Rev Turner Edwards. The troop marched to Halston, and then after manoeuvres the troops were entertained by Captain Mytton.[116]

Also, in 1797 the Shrewsbury Flax Mill was built by Bage on land previously owned by John Mytton. Artisan houses were built adjacent to the Flax Mill.[117]

In 1798 Captain John Mytton died and Lieutenant Lloyd resigned. The Adjutant G H Warrington was promoted to Captain and Cornet Venables became a Lieutenant. The new Cornet was J Rogers and A Davenport became Adjutant. Following an amendment of the Act of 1794 it was now possible that the deputy Lieutenants could dispense with the Provisional Cavalry and to substitute Yeomanry Cavalry in their place. At a meeting in the County convened by the High Sheriff, Mr Andrew Corbet, on 26 April 1798, it was resolved to make that substitution and so the Provisional Cavalry became the Yeomanry Cavalry.[118]

On 17 May 1799, a second troop of Rangers was raised by Mr Owen Ormsby of Porkington, he was made Major Commandant. Rev Turner Edwards became chaplain and Warrington, Venables, Rogers and Davenport were appointed to similar posts in this second troop.

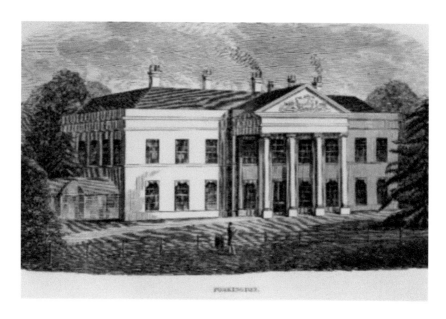

15. Porkington   Author`s Collection
Cathrall, William, *History of Oswestry* (Oswestry 1871)

MINIATURE OF JOHN MYTTON

16. John Mytton Esq of Halston   Author`s Collection

John (Mad Jack) Mytton MP (1796 - 1834)

As he was known as Jack he will be referred to as that in future pages. Jack was born at Halston, near Oswestry, Shropshire, on 30 September 1796, the only son of John Mytton (1768–1798) and Harriet Owen. On 21 May 1818 Jack married Harriet Emma Jones (1798-1820), the eldest daughter of Sir Thomas Tyrwhitt Jones, Bart of Stanley Hall, Shropshire. In the following year Harriet gave birth to a daughter, Harriet Emma Charlotte Mytton. Then at the age of just 22, on 2 July 1820, Jack`s wife Harriet Emma died. Before his wife`s death Jack was elected as MP for Shrewsbury in 1819. On 29 October 1821, Jack married his second wife Caroline Mallet Giffard, sixth daughter of Thomas Giffard, of Chillington Hall, Staffordshire. He was appointed. high-sheriff of Merioneth in 1821 and of Shropshire in 1823. Mayor of Oswestry in 1824/5.

Early Life

Jack`s mother had to bring him up on her own from the age of two, as his father had died in 1798, aged just 30. Jack got used to having his own way and was brought up without any restraint, and to say he was spoiled is an understatement. According to a neighbour, Sir Richard Puleston, Jack was the king of pickles and gave him the nickname `Mango`, which he lived up to for the rest of his life. Generous to his friends and acquaintances alike he did many good deeds, but it was his natural way with animals and his ability riding horses that marked him out as exceptional. He was known for the many tricks and jokes he played on his friends and acquaintances.[119]

In 1805, William Upton Wynne Owen, the son of Rev Edward Owen of Llanymawddy, Merioneth, chaplain at Halston, was appointed as Jack`s personal tutor. His new tutor was well qualified as he had matriculated at Jesus College, Oxford on 26

March 1794, aged 19, and he gained a BA in 1798 and an MA in 1800.

As many of the people close to Jack discovered knowing him made them a target of his incessant jokes, japes and pranks, for example, one morning his tutor found a black pony had been put into his bedroom.[120] In spite of the jokes, Jack and William Owen became close friends with common bonds of having a love of horses and their knowledge of the stud book. William continued to be the butt of Jack`s jokes and japes his goodwill was regularly tested, for example, one Sunday as William Owen was about to read a sermon, he discovered his sermon had been replaced by the Sporting Magazine.[121]

School Days

On 5 June 1807 Jack enrolled at Westminster, as a town boy, here he spent twice his yearly allowance of £400, which he was awarded when he was appointed a ward of Chancery. The next year at Halston, Jack became master of his own very mixed pack of hounds and hunted around the grounds of the estate with stable lads and servants.

Jack did well at Westminster as a sportsman and fighter, but in 1811, he was sent home, the polite expression for being expelled from School.[122] It is not surprising he became a noted boxer, when the culture of Westminster encouraged the "Noble Art of Self Defence" although his fighting style owed little to the science of the noble art. The boys used to take on locals at Scholar`s Green as recalled by some former pupils.

"What Old Westminster boy but would remember the battles of the Scholars' Green? In the old days there existed but a post and rail fence around it, and a short cut across it was frequently a temptation to the pedestrian; but woe to the trespasser if the boys

were there. At that time, when the noble art of self-defence was fashionable, the Westminster boy was proud of displaying his prowess on any such occasion. There were no police then, and the population of the town could not have been one-half if a third of the present. A street-keeper or Bow-Street officer generally contrived to keep out of the way, and so the fight went on uninterruptedly until satisfaction had been obtained. On some such occasions an obstinate 'coaly' has been known to exercise the active muscular powers of a King's Scholar for an hour or more. If Greek met not Greek, he nevertheless objected neither to coaly, baker, dustman, sweep, nor other if trespasser, without further fear of the disgrace, save that of being worsted in the encounter. "[123]

The following year, Jack went to Harrow and as he was quick to learn, he acquired a good knowledge of Latin and Greek. From then on he was always ready with an appropriate quotation from the Classical author`s. He was expelled for fighting after three terms, by which time he had fought eight pitch battles.[124]

But fighting and classics were not all Jack learned at school, all of the boys acquired skills of how to drink like a gentleman. They were supposed to be able to hold their alcohol, without displaying any ill effects. Gout and obesity were almost fashionable amongst the gentry at the time. The seeds were sown at school for the acute alcoholism that affected Jack for rest of his short life. His mother was not surprised to see him drink a bottle of port after dinner, as it was the done-thing, and she may have quietly approved, for a short while. However, she must have been concerned as she had also seen his temper. As mentioned previously he wanted his own way and was bad tempered if he did not get it. His temper got more out of control, he became violently extreme and this mood always followed his bouts of excessive drinking which must have included visits to the local taverns and bars in Oswestry and Shrewsbury. His appetite for port was such that he was drinking up to six bottles per day.[125]

After Jack left Harrow, he moved to a private tutor in Berkshire, but was later withdrawn; the reason was no surprise to some as he had knocked this tutor down. After this his friend and former tutor William Owen encouraged Jack to go to university. Jack agreed on condition that he would only read the *Racing Calendar* and the *Form Book*. The legend is that he ordered 3 pipes of port, a pipe being 55 dozen bottles, a total of 2,000 bottles to be sent ahead of his arrival. There is no evidence he ever matriculated at Cambridge and when asked a member of the records team confirmed there was no evidence recorded that he ever attended a lecture.[126]

Thus, his formal education had ceased. By that time, he had become impervious to advice and in spite of his quick wit and memory he did not read books or newspapers, only the aforementioned racing publications. His memory seemed to be exceptional as he only read business documents once, before signing them.

The Grand Tour

When the Peninsular War against France ended, the borders opened up and then, aged eighteen, he decided to go on the Grand Tour. Primarily for students who had completed their formal education, the Grand Tour was seen as a stepping stone to adulthood and an essential step to becoming a rounded gentleman. Similar to a gap year today, the object was to learn about other peoples, their customs and languages and this was achieved by various cultural activities. These included visiting museums and art galleries, by attending dance classes and going to riding schools, learning etiquette with the aim of acquiring a range of social skills appropriate for a young gentleman.

When free from parental control many young gentlemen took the opportunity to sow their wild oats, for example, in Paris with courtesans at The Louvre and in this Jack Mytton excelled.

When he returned home to Halston he was also welcomed back by the sporting fraternity and his old friends the bookmakers, card sharps, broken down jockeys and of course ladies of the Oswestry and Shrewsbury taverns.[127] He was followed by his acolytes shouting "here comes Mytton."[128] When he walked into a room he shouted "View Haloo" In the taverns he was king, and showed off his muscles, flex his pecs and was flattered by the tavern patrons.[129] Halston became an easy touch for scroungers, and was charitable to the local poor as each week a batch of bread was baked to give away at the gates.[130]

Military Service

On 18 March 1812, there was a reorganisation of the Oswestry Rangers. W Owen was commissioned as Major Commandant, John Hunt was appointed as Lieutenant and Jack took over as Captain. He may have had a feeling of pride at being part of this corps founded by his father, now eighty-nine strong rank and file with seven officers.[131]

The Prince Regent gave consent for the two troops of Oswestry Rangers to be merged into the North Shropshire Yeomanry Cavalry, with Major Owen being promoted to Lieutenant Colonel in 1814.[132] This new body included; The Shropshire Yeomanry Cavalry, the Pimhill Light Horse and the Market Drayton Troop. Jack retained his Captaincy and on 2 June 1814 the newly amalgamated corps, of 430 rank and file and 28 officers, met at Shrewsbury to take part in a procession organised to welcome home General Lord Hill from his service with the Duke of Wellington.[133]

Jack decided to extend his military experience and on 30 May 1816 he became a cornet in the 7th Hussars. He was posted to the army of occupation in St Omar in France, under the Duke of Wellington. Jack took John, his servant, with him. As there was not much military activity other than drilling and training, he spent much time racing, gambling and losing money heavily. He bought a horse, with only one eye, which became one of his favourite hunters, named Baronet and they hunted with the Duke of Wellington`s pack in France. Jack left the army the following year, but continued in the North Shropshire Yeomanry Cavalry and was promoted to major in 1822, a rank he held until his death.

The duties of the North Shropshire Yeomanry Cavalry included assembling, exercising, training and an annual permanent duty of seven or eight days in various towns around Shropshire. For example, in 1830 the regiment assembled for eight days permanent duty at Market Drayton. General Lord Hill Commander in Chief of the forces was on the ground in civilian clothing. Following an inspection by Lieutenant Colonel Townsend of the 14th regiment of Dragoons, a ball was held in the evening of the seventh day. On the ninth day the whole regiment was entertained at Hawkstone to a cold collation by Sir Rowland Hill.[134]

Jack comes of age on 30 September 1817

As one of the leading local gentry Jack`s twenty-first birthday was celebrated throughout Shropshire and beyond. Just as a Royal wedding is an excuse for a community party so it was with Jack`s twenty-first. Almost everyone in Shropshire had a reason to be involved and they had a full day and night of celebration.

The day began early with cannon being fired and peals of different bells rang out across the County and continued throughout the day. It was an excuse for many parties held throughout the County and many well-wishers headed for Halston Hall.

The townspeople celebrated too. The hotels and dining establishments in Shrewsbury were busy with groups of friends who dined and wined at their favourite places including the Lion Hotel, the Talbot, the Elephant and Castle and the Cock Inn.

In Ellesmere the inhabitants all gave their good wishes to the Mytton family. The guests of Mr Death of the Bridgewater Arms took part of the most excellent dinner, including game, venison and every delicacy of the seas. Then at the very moment they were drinking a bumper toast to the health of Mr Mytton they were all gratified to see that worthy gentleman himself drive past the house.

A twenty-one-gun salute was sounded at 11 o`clock and in the local villages around Halston, in Whittington and St Martins, the bells rang out and many changes were rung. A fine ox and two sheep were roasted on a wagon with a barrel of good old stingo.[135] Bands played and flags with arms were taken to Whittington, where a barrel of ale was drawn and drunk. Others had an excellent dinner at the Boot Inn, where good company and merry making was the order of the day. From there many people went off to join the festivities of the day at Halston.

At Halston preparations had been going on for weeks to be ready for the many guests from Shropshire and neighbouring counties, who had been invited for the day. They were welcomed by the road from Whittington to the house lighted with lamps. The guests met in the ballroom which had been decorated with leaves of laurel flowers. A temporary portico was erected near the entrance of the house, it was brilliantly illuminated and it had a magnificent appearance. A grand display of fireworks took place. It was estimated that the number of people exceeded 7,000.[136]

Physical characteristics

Nimrod, the pen name adopted by Charles James Apperley, his friend and biographer, described Jack as having both in person and mind the gifts of nature amply bestowed upon him with animal faculties to a degree seldom witnessed. His biceps were larger than Jackson's, a celebrated pugilist, with every other part of his body equally powerful. He had bull-dog courage and his prowess in a fight was well known although he only stood about five feet nine inches, his weight varied between eleven to thirteen stone. His iron constitution was impervious to cold. Probably because of his being born prematurely, at seven months, he was slightly deaf. He was stocky and pugnacious with a pleasing countenance rather than a handsome face, not unattractive to women. He carried on many liaisons in his life before and after his marriages, although later he became overweight and was described as a physical wreck.[137]

Nimrod described Jack as wearing the thinnest and finest silk stockings with very fine thin shoes and boots, all London made, which were very light and got destroyed by his taking long walks over the county, in winter he rarely had dry feet. Jack would ride several times in a week sometimes to places fifty miles away from Halston and return home for dinner. His hunting breeches were without lining. He wore a small waistcoat, always open at the front from the second lowest button. In winter his shooting outfit was a light jacket, white linen trousers without lining and he wore no underwear. He never carried nor needed a pocket handkerchief and rarely wore gloves. He always knew the hour although he never wore a watch. Nimrod counted the contents of Jack's wardrobe at Halston, as having 152 pairs of breeches and trousers with appropriate accompaniment of coats and waistcoats. Whilst his drinking was legendary and in 4-6 bottles of port there were plenty of calories say 4000-6000 per day his diet was not recorded, but he enjoyed eating filbert nuts as reported by Nimrod. On one occasion he and a friend left London in a coach and consumed between them eighteen pounds of filberts and at the end of the trip they were up to their knees in shells.[138]

Marriage to Harriet Emma Jones

His marriage was a military and society highlight of the year. On 21 May 1818, at St George`s Church, Hanover Square, London, Jack married Harriet Emma Jones, the eldest daughter of the late Sir Thomas Tyrwhitt Jones, Bart of Stanley Hall, Shropshire. The bridegroom was attended by the Earl of Uxbridge, The Earl of Denbigh, Sir Watkin Williams Wynn, Bart, Col Sir Edward Kerrison. The guests included the Duchess of Marlborough and Lady Caroline Churchill, Sir John and Lady Dashwood, Sir Edward and Lady Kerrison, Lord and Lady Say and Sale, the Marquess of Blandford and Lord Charles Churchill, and many other persons of distinction. The elegant wedding breakfast was taken at the home of Lady Jones in New Norfolk St, after which the happy couple left for the seat of the Duke of Marlborough at Blenheim.

The Marriage settlement listed the rental value of property in Whittington and Oswestry as £3,507/16s/0d; Habberley and Pulverbatch £777/15s/ 6d; Mowthy and Dinas Mowdy £790/12s/0d; Shrewsbury £1,599/5s/ 10d, a total of £6,676 per annum.[139]

Jack`s wife Emma was described as delicate and did not enjoy good health and probably had a nervous disposition. He did not enjoy her chatter and gossip, which got on his nerves and it was his justification to go back to the Shrewsbury Inns. Emma got on well with Jack`s mother, she had assisted in a reconciliation between the couple and he came home for a short while, with the prospect of an heir Jack was encouraged to remain close to home. But when Emma gave birth to a girl, Harriet Emma Charlotte (1819–1885) Jack was beside himself with disappointment, although he got over it and eventually did take to his daughter.

Engages with politics and becomes MP for Shrewsbury

Mytton was open-handed and generous with money, as the Shrewsbury voters found when he bribed them before the 1819 by-election. However, having offered himself as a candidate for the Tory contingent and started to canvas support, a number of respectable freemen did not consider him a fit and discreet person to represent the Borough. As a result, a meeting was called at the Talbot Inn, where it was agreed to ask Panton Corbett Esq if he would stand as a candidate against Mytton.

When nominations were heard in the Guildhall on 15 May 1819, following the reading of the Writ and the Statute Against Bribery John Cresset Pelham proposed Jack Mytton as being a fit and proper person to represent Shrewsbury this was seconded by Col Burgh Leighton. Then W. Cludde Esq proposed and John Beck seconded the motion that Panton Corbett be adopted as a candidate.

The election began with the first of seven days of voting on Monday 17 May 1819, with Mytton supporters using tactics to limit Panton Corbett`s campaign. But in the afternoon matters got worse. At around 5.00pm, upward of 150 men, armed with bludgeons, entered Shrewsbury and attacked Panton Corbett and his supporters as they were returning to their headquarters.

As a result of this and other intimidation on Tuesday 18 May at 5pm Panton Corbett was forced to retire from the contest. He was held in high respect in the eyes of the general public and he said of his supporters they did not barter their freedom for ale or money. The Poll Book of the 1819 election records that Jack recorded 384 votes and Panton Corbett 287.[140] This was not the end of Panton Corbett's political career as he served as MP for Shrewsbury from 1820-30.[141]

Mytton's bribe involved extensive hospitality and other favours and it worked, as enough voters were convinced, and he was elected as an MP.[142] It is was said to have cost him £10,000. In the run up to the election an opposing candidate had a fighting champion who would take on all comers, Jack accepted the challenge and thrashed him, Jack then pushed some money into his fist to make him comfortable for the evening. Following the success of his election victory he was being Chaired home from the hustings on a cart when he threw himself through the window of the Lion Inn without any concern for his own safety.[143]

Jack is recorded as having paid one visit to Westminster, but he was said to have left after half-an-hour from boredom and restlessness, he seemed unable to sit anywhere for long and possibly because of his deafness, he may not have heard much of the business. His name appeared in the majority for the foreign enlistment bill on 10 June.[144] He failed to stand at the next general election in 1820, perhaps owing to financial troubles. A few years later Mytton, though impoverished, was thinking to stand again in 1825-6. He supported plans for lowering the town walls and creating public gardens and walkways along the Severn and in the grounds of the Castle.[145]

Jack`s relationship with Emma

Jack`s relationship with Emma throws up a number of stories which have become legendary and illustrate the difference in their personalities. It has been suggested he treated her insensitively, harshly and badly.

Whilst Jack he was out hunting or about-town he made Emma stay at home. He did not encourage visitors to Halston and Emma became isolated. The story was told that he pushed her into the Lake but he claimed she was only in up to her toes in about 2 inches of water. Another story was that he locked her in the kennels with the hounds, but it transpired she was behind Jack and he claimed he had not heard her and he duly shut her in for a few seconds. Another story was that Jack mistreated her lap dog by throwing it onto a fire, but he explained that he playfully threw the dog up in the air and caught it and the butler caused a fuss as he said to be careful that the dog will end up in the fire.

Emma became ill with consumption, as tuberculosis was known as in Victorian times, and her doctor suggested a visit to the hot springs of Clifton near Bristol which may have helped alleviate her symptoms. An effective treatment was not available at the time and without antibiotics Emma wasted away and died on 2 July 1820, at the age of just 22.

Money

His annual income would have been substantial for the time with his Shropshire and Montgomeryshire estates producing almost £5,000 a year, or £287,000 a year in spending power in 2021.[146] The settlement on his marriage added to his income.

When he came of age he had access to the capital, which he had inherited from his father`s estate, he found new popularity and new so-called friends in the ale houses of Shrewsbury and Oswestry and as his own consumption of alcohol was prodigious the money flowed out. His interests and hobbies were all expensive and included hunting, shooting, fishing, horse racing, cock fighting and gambling. As mentioned previously his clothing and footwear was of the finest quality being London made and naturally the most expensive.

He was careless with the money he borrowed. On one occasion Jack borrowed £10,000 on an annuity paying a high interest rate, he lent £9,000 of it to a friend who disappeared and was never seen in Europe again.[147]

Jack ensured that trees were planted on the estate in abundance, firstly to replace those used on the estate for agricultural and domestic purposes and secondly to provide excellent cover for game. Jack`s recruitment policies were quite unusual as you would expect. The Estate needed to employ gamekeepers to look after and protect the game birds from poachers. On one occasion he told the applicant to watch for a sweep and if he saw him to thrash him to stop him returning. The candidate waited and the sweep appeared and the fight began, the sweep was duly thrashed and the new gamekeeper was hired. It turned out later that Jack was in disguise as the sweep and he wanted to ensure first-hand that the gamekeeper was up to the job.

17. Mytton takes a drop "As high as a House" Author's collection
Illustration by Henry Alken, *Memoirs of the Life of the Late John
Mytton Esq of Halston* (London-1903)

Horseman Extraordinary

Jack's national fame was due to his horse-riding skills which
were legendary. He was an excellent horseman with prodigious
strength which helped the horses get over jumps that they
probably would not have been able to manage with an average
rider.

He attempted ground that others avoided and once rode at
break neck speed over a rabbit warren until inevitably the horse
fell. He was said to have a way with animals and learned to ride
from an early age, he hunted a pack of mixed breed hounds
around the estate at Halston. This stood him in good stead when
he was a master of foxhounds from 1818 to 1821. He spent large
amounts on hounds which he maintained at his own expense and

he hunted regularly in two counties.[148] This vast area extended from Halston in Shropshire into Staffordshire and included what was later the country of the Albrighton hunt. Jack spent hours in the saddle. If he went to a meet starting in Shifnal, for example, he had to ride there in the morning, he would hunt all day and then ride back to Halston in the evening. It was estimated he would have covered 80 miles during some days.

18. "A Squire-trap, by Jove" cries Mytton   Author`s Collection
Illustration by Henry Alken, *Memoirs of the Life of the Late John Mytton Esq of Halston* (London-1903)

Extraordinary Fox Chase

In November 1818 Jack was hunting in North Shropshire on Twemlow Moor, when after a two-hour run, the fox led them into Whitchurch, but at Green End a crowd turned the fox over towards the Town Pool Meadow. Here the fox rested briefly in a couple of gardens before he entered through the open door of a house to the consternation of the owner. The fox was chased upstairs and hid in a cupboard, pursued by the hounds and several huntsmen, headed by Lord Hill, and the fox was taken. Jack had to pay out money to compensate the somewhat shocked and elderly owner a Miss Langford.[149]

Later in the 1820s, he hunted around Halston with a pack of hounds and harriers bought from Cressett Pelham. This additional pack may have created another legend that Jack had two thousand dogs. An average pack of hounds would be twenty to thirty couples as if hunted in greater numbers they would become unmanageable. Two thousand dogs would require huge quantities of feed, exercise and training.

19. Well done, Neck or Nothing!   Author's collection
Illustration by Henry Alken, *Memoirs of the Life of the Late John Mytton Esq of Halston* (London-1903)

For an example of his skill, whilst recovering from a fall with his right arm in a sling, he was hunting with Sir Bellingham Graham`s hounds and he rode Baronet over the Lord Berwick`s park paling at Attingham Park, Atcham, near Shrewsbury. This astonished everyone and Sir Bellingham exclaimed "Well done Neck or Nothing! You are not a bad one to breed from."[150]

20. Baronet clears the Perry   Author`s Collection
Illustration by Henry Alken, *Memoirs of the Life of the Late John Mytton Esq of Halston* (London-1903)

One of his favourite horses was Baronet, bought when stationed with the Army in France, and then went on to carry Jack for nine hunting seasons. They were a great team and managed to jump over the river Perry which ran through the estate, the leap was measured at over 9 yards.[151]

On another day on a run approaching Haughmond Hill the field was held up when they arrived at the River Severn, near the Uppington Ferry. Without hesitation Jack shouted," Let all who call themselves sportsmen follow me." He drove his horse into the Severn, gained the opposite bank and caught up with the hounds.

Shavington Day

A special day in the hunting calendar of Cheshire, Shropshire and Staffordshire was "The Shavington Day", a trial of speed, nose and bottom. The contestants were the fox-hounds of Sir Harry Mainwaring of Peover Hall, Cheshire, known as the Cheshire Hounds; the pack kept by Sir Edward Smythe, of Acton Burnell Park, Mr Smythe Owen of Condover Hall and Mr Lloyd of Aston Hall, Salop, known as the Shropshire Hounds and that of Mr Wicksted whose kennel was at Betley, near Woore in Staffordshire.

21. "Now for the honour of Shropshire."   Author`s Collection
Illustration by Henry Alken, *Memoirs of the Life of the Late John Mytton Esq of Halston* (London-1903)

Nimrod estimated there were a thousand horsemen in the field with about seven hundred in scarlet, without counting supporters and others on horseback and in carriages. The meeting place was Shavington Hall, in Cheshire, the seat of an Irish nobleman Viscount Kilmorey.

The trial required six couples out of each pack to be selected and each were attended by their best huntsman, and the leading huntsman was Will Head, the man with local knowledge. Mytton had brought one of his best hunters Hit-or-Miss, a mare who was very fast and had excellent stamina.

After a good chase Mytton got to the front, but coming to a deep sunk fence, a ha-ha, with a high stiff rail on the rising side, he went for it, his mare fell and he had a severe fall. Another horse landed on top of him and crushed him. The fall had shaken him but he remounted and had to go bareheaded, his hat having been severely damaged in the accident. Jack had to be content with following the leader until the end of the day.[152]

As he was keen on hunting, Jack became enthusiastic to get involved with horse racing and leaping. He competed as a rider and later as an owner from 1817 to 1830. He started a racing stables and bought *Hazard* and *Neck or Nothing* and entered races at Oswestry. His horse *Langolee* won a match at Shrewsbury and he increased the stable to eight. His colours were green and white with a black cap. In 1819 the stables were moved to Delamere Forest and it was following this move that he met Charles James Apperley.

Apperley was born in Plasgronow, Denbighshire, in 1778 of an old Herefordshire family. In 1790 he was educated at Rugby and was a cousin of Mr Owen, a kindred spirit of Jack`s with a love of horses and an expensive lifestyle but without the income to support it. He had joined the Army in 1798 and he became an expert horseman, and had hunted since he was twelve years old. At one stage he moved to Leicestershire so he could hunt with the Quorn, but now having left the Army, he was in an impoverished state and latched on to the free ride that being a friend of Jack's offered. He was good company and made a little money dealing horses.

He moved to live at Brewood in Staffordshire and became acquainted with the Giffards of Chillington Hall. It was Apperley who introduced Jack to the family and he got on well with Mr Giffard and his sons, as they were all sporting men. Apperley thought Jack and Caroline Giffard might make a suitable match, and Jack, in need of a son and heir, became interested in his friend's recommendation

22. Chillington Hall   Author's Photograph

It was that on 29 October 1821, Jack married his second wife Caroline Mallet Giffard, sixth daughter of Thomas Giffard, of Chillington Hall, Staffordshire. The marriage settlement provided `£500 in the nature of Pin Money` for Caroline.[153] Although Jack was disappointed again when their first child and their only daughter was born in 1822, Barbara Augusta Mytton, he was able to celebrate when John Fox Fitz Giffard Mytton (1823-1875) was born as his first son and heir. Two years later Charles Orville Mytton (1825-1834) was born, but he died aged 9 in 1834. The same year his younger brother Euphrates Henry (1826-1834) died. The couple's last child was William Harper Mytton (1827-1896) survived and became a Captain in the Royal Artillery.

Shortly after the wedding Apperley moved to London and became a writer for the *Sporting Magazine* using the pseudonym Nimrod, and remained the hunting correspondent until the owner died in 1829 and the magazine closed.[154]

Responsibilities

After his second wedding Jack seemed to settle down for a while and appeared to accept some of the responsibilities of a gentleman in his position. He was appointed high-sheriff of Merioneth in 1821 and of Shropshire in 1823. He was promoted to major of the North Shropshire Yeomanry Cavalry on 1 June 1822, became treasurer of the Royal Shrewsbury Infirmary and in 1924/5 he was elected mayor of Oswestry.[155] Caroline was a more robust character than the late Emma and would share Jacks jokes and although the marriage ended in tears, at the start they appeared to work well together.

Jack began to go off the rails again and had numerous affairs, which were the subject of much local gossip and amusement. According to Nimrod, Jack was the best farmer in this part of the county having three to four hundred acres of land under cultivation. He was also a successful maltster and at one of Shropshire's agricultural shows he gained several prizes for clean crops of grain, other than one of his fields of barley, which the judges found it contained 'wild oats'. Because of his reputation and number of affairs the judges' comments caused much amusement with the farmers gathered at the prize-giving.

Jack continued to invest heavily in horses but was not a successful breeder. He met John Beardsworth, a horse dealer from Birmingham, and they formed an informal partnership in which Beardsworth generally sold poor horses for high prices to Jack. Although he was very successful with a horse named Euphrates that won a few races, then as now racehorse ownership was an expensive hobby and few even covered their costs and few had profitable seasons. The numbers of horses in the racing stable increased to fifteen to twenty horses with brood mares and young things about thirty-six horses to feed, exercise and keep healthy.[156] Jack spent money without a second thought, some trophies were won but at enormous cost. One of the main costs of racing was the wagers placed on the horses by the owners, good horses and good jockeys were needed to win races and to win the wagers. Cock fighting was an important part of many race meetings and yet another opportunity to make wagers and to lose even more money.

Shooting

Jack was a first-class marksman with a rifle and pistol as told by Nimrod, he was known to be able to hit the edge of a razor at a distance of 30 yards and occasionally split the ball. He would also demonstrate his accuracy by crossing the yard at Halston and shoot from the iron gates on the drive to the coal house wall, a distance of fifty-five yards and put a ball through the peg-hole of a trimmer used in pike fishing. The trimmer cork aperture was covered with white paper and no more than an inch and a half in diameter. This was done with his rifle to his shoulder and not on a rest. Many other stories tell of his skill including putting a ball through a man's hat whilst on his head. It was said his skill comes from his shooting rats with a rifle from the top of his house.

Not one to do things he enjoyed by half; Jack ensured a plentiful supply of game birds at Halston where every species of game bird was made available for the sport. One invoice he paid to a London game dealer was for £1,500 for pheasants and foxes to help fill three miles of plantation with game. He had up to fifty labourers employed in the estate and local keepers, on neighbouring estates, were commissioned to save all the vermin they trapped to be brought to Halston. These men brought sacks of wild animals including badgers, stoats and polecats to fill the plantations with live targets.[157]

His appetite appeared never satisfied when it came to quantities of game shot. The average number for pheasants totalled twelve hundred braces, for hares from fifteen hundred to two thousand and of partridges they were out of number. In addition, there were also a good number of wild fowl and excellent fishing, a special feature of the well-stocked Halston estate included a heronry.

Jack set himself targets for numbers bagged and of partridge he aimed for fifty on the first day of the season. On one occasion in winter with his brother-in-law, Mr Walter Giffard of Chillington, they took the field at eleven o clock and the two of them bagged over six hundred head of game. In addition to Halston, the moors on the Merionethshire estate provided opportunities for target practice as they were stocked with grouse. Thirty braces being the average bag for a day on the moors at Mowddy, and the shooting parties produced an income of £800 annually.[158]

He would sometimes follow wildfowl at night and in hard weather. It is said he once stripped naked to follow some duck over the ice, or in his night shirt, as shown in the later Victorian edition of his biography published in 1903.

23. Duck shooting by moonlight   Author's Collection
Illustration by Henry Alken, *Memoirs of the Life of the Late John Mytton Esq of Halston* (London-1903)

Cricket

He played other sports including cricket which was becoming popular as he grew up. The first cricket match in Shropshire was a match of the Shrewsbury Cricket Society in August 1794 on Kingsland.[159] In 1817 matches were played at Underdale, Shrewsbury and Weston near Oswestry between the Gentlemen of Shropshire and the Gentlemen of Oswestry. The Shropshire team included J Cresset Pelham, Henry Lyster of Rowton, Robert Burton of Longner and other members of the Atcham Club. The Oswestry team had as captain W Ormesby-Gore, other players included R A Slaney of Walford, the Revd J Russell and Jack Mytton who were members of Oswestry Cricket Club and they were playing regularly at Weston by 1821.[160] Matches in 1817 may have led to the formation of a county team, for in 1818 the Gentlemen of Shropshire played against the Gentlemen of

Cheshire, another match was played in 1820, the Atcham club styled itself The Shropshire Cricket Club.[161] Cricket bats and balls were listed in the final sale of John Mytton`s belongings in 1831.

Raising Funds by Selling and Mortgaging properties

Starting on the day of his majority he began raising money on properties he owned either by sale or by mortgage. These were the properties built up by previous generations. By 1819 many properties were heavily mortgaged and loans on his personal security were hard to find. The mortgaging and re-mortgaging of property continued, for example, on 25 March 1821 Mr & Mrs Parr lent £6,500 secured on mortgage to John Mytton, later a further £4,000 was lent on mortgage by Mr & Mrs Parr.[162]

"On 5 May 1821 Dr Robert Darwin paid £2,691/11s/ 9d to John Mytton of lawful money of Great Britain current in England for Sparkes`s Field, just over 5 acres, Bishops Land just over 7acres and Far Bishops Land just over 6 acres. Near Frankwell, one of the suburbs of Shrewsbury together with all and single Edifices, Buildings, hedges, ditches, fences, trees, woods, under woods, Ways, Water, Water-Courses, Roads, paths, passages, Easements, Mines, Minerals, Quarries, profits, privileges, emolument's, hereditaments and Appurtenances."[163]

As the loans and mortgages were not repaid in the normal way so land and property had to be sold to repay the bills and to meet the demands from his creditors. An example of this was the 3 Day Sale by the auctioneer Perry, from 25 November 1824, of property in Frankwell, Shelton & Crowmeole, Bicton and 16 dwelling houses in Castle Foregate. About 80 properties were offered for sale and about £80,000 was received excluding sales of timber. Stamp duty was payable by purchasers at the rate of 7d per £100. The sale included the east part of the Shrewsbury Race

Ground, the Four Crosses public house in Bicton and The Nags Head in Montford Bridge.[164]

Some of the property in Crowmeole had been held by the Myttons since 1428, his solicitor commented "that these properties had been in the family a long time" Jack replied "Well it is quite time they were out of it", the sales continued until there were no more to sell. Halston could not be sold as it was entailed, and was held in trust for Jack`s surviving heir.

Jack tried to borrow money from friends and acquaintances. As an example, in a letter to John Mott of the Close, Lichfield. Jack explained he had been trying to sell a property and raise money and said that he would like to borrow £2,000 and repay in twelve months via a bond. He was so desperate he asked that the reply should go direct to Halston, Oswestry and not Salop as it makes a difference as he was pressed for time.[165]

Practical Jokes or Impractical?

He was a man of great physical strength and foolhardy courage, with a strong taste for practical jokes. He was a splendid shot and a daring horseman. There are numerous stories of his recklessness. He is said to have galloped at full speed over a rabbit warren just to see if his horse would fall, which it did and rolled over him.

He was dining at Mr Walford`s at Cronkhill as the wine flowed the conversation moved to the difficulty of controlling the lead horse in a tandem gig. Jack said he would have no problem controlling his gig across country to the turnpike half a mile away across country. He offered a bet of £25 to all takers. Twelve men with lanterns illuminated the route across a sunk fence, three yards wide; a broad deep drain; and two stiff quick fences, with ditches on the far side. The first sunken fence was surmounted and whipped the horses up the other side. Jack took the next obstacle the broad deep drain at such a pace that it was cleared by a yard, but he was pitched on the wheelers back. He recovered his seat and took the last two fences with ease and arrived at the turnpike to claim the £150 that had been wagered against him.[166] All these stories built the legend of Mad Jack and having earned it he maintained his reputation for crazy and mad stunts with a complete disregard for his own health or safety.

24. Cross Country night ride for a wager   Author`s Collection
Illustration by Henry Alken, *Memoirs of the Life of the Late John Mytton Esq of Halston* (London-1903)

25. Never Upset in a Gig?   Author`s Collection
Illustration by Henry Alken, *Memoirs of the Life of the Late John Mytton Esq of Halston* (London-1903)

     A horse dealer found out what a prankster Jack was when having a lift with Jack driving. He told Jack he had never had an accident in a gig and almost immediately Jack contrived to turn the gig over and they both fell out. Another friend George Underhill was owed money and went to Jack to demand payment. Jack wrote out a note handed it to George to take for payment to the address of a banker in Shrewsbury. The banker was also manager of the Asylum who was startled to read the note which said "Admit the Bearer to The Asylum." [167] On another occasion when George drank too much and stayed at Halston over-night he woke to find a bulldog and a bear in his bed.

26. Stand and deliver.   Authors Collection
Illustration by Henry Alken, *Memoirs of the Life of the Late John Mytton Esq of Halston* (London-1903)

Disguised as a highwayman, complete with his blazing pistols with blanks, he ambushed a doctor and a parson who had just been visiting Halston and chased them to Oswestry. On another night he ambushed his own butler, who had boasted he would never be robbed of the money he regularly carried for Jack. As the butler was returning with some money from an agent. Jack in disguise pointed a pistol and the butler gave up the cash and his watch without any resistance.

27." I wonder whether he is a good timber jumper?"
Author's Collection   Illustration by Henry Alken in *Memoirs of the Life of the Late John Mytton Esq of Halston* (London-1903)

Jack placed an order with a local horse dealer named Clarke, of Meole, for some carriage horses. Putting the horses into a tandem gig he asked the dealer if he would make a good leader? Then with the dealer sitting beside him he asked if he was a good timber jumper? The dealer expressed some doubts and Jack said "We will try him!" Jack closed the turn-pike gate, at Hanwood, then giving the lead horse its head and a whip on his flank, they were off, the horse sailed over with some style leaving the other horse, Mytton, the dealer and the gig on the other side. Although the occupants survived the gig was severely damaged.

28. Light come light go. (Easy come Easy go)
Author's Collection   Illustration by Henry Alken in *Memoirs of the Life of the Late John Mytton Esq of Halston* (London-1903)

Jack spent large amounts on post-horses and tipped the post boys generously. Post horses and riders were available at inns and stations on the post roads to make deliveries of post and urgent items. They were also available for hire by travellers and used by the wealthy as taxis. One event recalled by Nimrod was a return journey from Warwick races via a stop off in Birmingham when Jack and his companion took the post boys places and drive at a very fast pace to Halston. There was a large reward which went someway to compensate the boys for their ordeal.

On another occasion when returning home from the races at Doncaster he was counting money held in his travelling writing desk. It was an unusually large amount as he had recently broken the bank in a London gambling hell. He was on his own and fell asleep. A gale blew up and as the windows were down a great amount disappeared into the night, Jack commented "Light come; light go.[169]

One of these adventures had serious consequences, when returning home in a coach with others, from the races in Wolverhampton in 1826. Jack got impatient with the speed of the coach and mounted the box took the reins and gave the offside horse a slash with the whip just as they were going around a bend. The sudden acceleration caused the coach to overturn and threw the remaining passengers over a hedge into a field. One of the passengers Mr Boycott of Rudge Hall, was seriously injured and subsequently died.

29. Jack Greets Lord Derby   Author`s Collection
Illustration by Henry Alken, *Memoirs of the Life of the Late John Mytton Esq of Halston* (London-1903)

When in London during the hunting season he decided to go to see Lord Derby`s Stag Hounds and to most of the throng he was a stranger, and they thought Jack might be a local tailor. He must have enjoyed the moment when Lord Derby`s carriage drove up and Lord Stanley exclaimed "Mytton who would have thought of seeing you here?" To which Jack replied, "To tell you the truth Stanley, I have ridden over many a good fellow in my own country, but I never rode over a Cockney, and I am come here today for that sole purpose."[170]

30. "Tally Ho", a new hunter ridden into the drawing room Author`s Collection   Illustration by Henry Alken, *Memoirs of the Life of the Late John Mytton Esq of Halston* (London-1903)

Jack once rode a bear into his drawing room in full hunting costume. "The bear carried him very quietly for a time; but on being pricked by the spur he bit his rider through the calf of his leg."[171]

Marriage to Caroline Giffard

Caroline loved Jack in spite of all his issues and dutifully had five children with him up to 1827, by which time his decline was becoming obvious. When visiting Halston his friend Nimrod was shocked to see his condition and thought he was not long for this world and penned Jack`s epitaph.

> *"Here lies John Mytton, his short career is past.*
> *The pace was quick and therefore could not last.*
> *From end to end he went on errant burst,*
> *Determined to be nowhere or first."*

When Nimrod talked with Caroline, she appeared to accept her lot. She seldom left the confines of Halston and did not appear socially with her husband because Jack would not take her to any of the local society balls or other charitable and social events, which was the case with Emma his first wife.

Caroline was worried about the lack of money but Jack continued his spending. He scorned advice from his agent when he suggested via Nimrod he could save his estate by living on £6,000 per annum. Nimrod recalls Jack`s reply "You may tell Longueville to keep his advice to himself, for I would not give a d----n to live on six thousand a year."[172]

Jack continued to ride and had a serious accident in April when his horse fell and rolled on top of him breaking six ribs. His horses had some success and he seemed to enjoy the company of his children but his short attention span seemed only to be satisfied by more alcohol. At the end of the 1828/9 season, he rode in the Shavington Day, and was leading the chase until he came to a sunken fence with a high rail on the take-off side, they fell and Jack was stunned and winded, then another horse landed on him and kicked in the head and chest and cut in the face. This was to be Jack's last time at Shavington and he took some time to recover. He spent time with Beardsworth gambling and drinking in Birmingham spending money he did not have. [173]

Inordinately convivial, Jack Mytton was said to drink from four to six bottles of port each day, beginning in the morning while shaving, and he eventually lived in a "nearly constant state of intoxication." Nimrod notes that one of Jack's oldest friends made an affidavit that Mytton had been drunk for twelve successive years! [174]

The cumulative effect was catching up with Jack, he had episodes of depression and delusions, he started attacking people and he despaired. He spent months wandering aimlessly visiting familiar haunts and travelled to London then almost immediately wanted to go home. He called at Chillington where the Giffard family sent him away as they had heard from Caroline of Jacks cruelty. Returning to Halston he calmed down for a few days but then on 14 October he flared up into a blazing rage and savagely attacked Caroline and she was saved by the intervention of their servants. She left with the children for the safety of Chillington. In November a Bill of Complaints against Jack was heard in the Chancery Division and it was granted to Caroline. She remained at Chillington, where she was under her brother's protection. [175]

In May Jack chose to stand to represent Shropshire in Parliament, surprisingly as a supporter of the Grey ministry's Reform Bill at the general election. The early result in the Oswestry Hundred showed Jack with 172 votes was leading by 3 from Sir Rowland Hill, with Mr William Lloyd on 165 and Cressett Pelham tailed off with 25. The overall total did not match the Oswestry result, which was a victory for Sir Rowland Hill with 1824 votes, with Cressett Pelham second with 1355, William Lloyd third with 828 votes. [176] Jacks local support was not matched in the County among the independent freeholders, who disliked "seeing a gentleman sink in the social scale", and he came bottom of the poll with 392 votes.[177]

Six months later, in November, he fled from his creditors and went to Calais, on his way he met a lady on London Bridge and offered her £500 to go with him to France, she never got her money but stayed with him for a while. By this time, he had spent his entire fortune and without security he was unable to borrow any more money. When the creditors finally ran out of patience and no one would advance him credit the contents of Halston were auctioned on 10 April 1831. His former business partner, John Beardsworth bought a large number of the effects of Halston. A couple of years later Beardsworth bought the Lordship of the Manor and lands at Mawddwy, he then passed them to his son-in-law John Bird and he sold them on to Sir Edmund Buckley.

In France he met up with Nimrod who had gone to write and to avoid his own creditors. Whilst in France Jack made a fatal mistake, he tried to frighten away hiccups by setting fire to his nightshirt. The hiccups went, but he was left with severe burns which hastened his final decline. Nimrod nursed and looked after him but Jack never fully recovered. His expensive lifestyle could not be maintained and with no more assets to sell his wit, charm, health and wealth were all dissipated he fell into a terminal and painful decline.

His strong constitution kept him alive for three more years, he had to drink more brandy to alleviate the pain from his burns and his swollen legs. Jack crossed the channel for the last time and was committed to the debtors King's-bench prison, Southwark.

31. Frighten away the hiccups   Author`s Collection
Illustration by Henry Alken in *Memoirs of the Life of the Late John Mytton Esq of Halston* (London-1903)

He died in the arms of his mother, on 29 March 1834 and The Times reported his death on Wednesday 2 April 1834.

"On Monday an inquest was held in the Kings Bench Prison on the body of John Mytton, Esq, who died there on the preceding Saturday. The deceased inherited considerable estates in the counties of Salop and Merioneth, for both he served the office of High Sheriff, and represented the borough of Shrewsbury in Parliament. His munificence and eccentric gaieties obtained him great notoriety in the sporting and gay circles, both in England and on the Continent. Two medical attendants stated that the immediate course of death was disease of the brain (delirium tremens), brought about by the excessive use of spirituous liquors. He was in his 38th year. Verdict, `Natural death`."[178]

After Jack`s Death

His dying revived public affection for him, and on 9 April 1834, a half-mile procession of tenants, friends, and yeomanry troops escorted his body the last five miles to Halston Chapel. Where, in the presence of perhaps 2000 – 3000 onlookers, he was buried in the family vault. Subsequently, his second wife, Caroline, in spite of her appalling treatment and her escape from Halston, chose to be buried next to him when her time came.

Halston passed to his son and heir John Fox Fitz Giffard Mytton (1823-1875) the only one of Jack and Caroline`s five children to pass the age of fifty. He inherited his father`s expensive tastes and had to sell the remaining Habberley property in 1846. In the following year having removed the entail on Halston, the family seat since 1549, was sold.

In 1847 Halston was purchased by Edmund Wright of Mauldeth Hall, Manchester (W. Mate, Shropshire Historical. Descriptive. Biographical (1906)145), the house was enlarged and underwent further improvement in the following years.

The Census,1871, for Halston Hall shows the five family members as Edmund Wright aged 57, shown as a Justice of the Peace; his wife Helen aged 51; daughter Helen aged 31; daughter Louisa aged 26; son Charles Henry aged 19 and son John Henry. The staff of eighteen members were James Babington aged 60 is shown as tutor, and the Edward Day was the butler aged 64, there were 2 footmen, 2 grooms, 1 house keeper 1 cook, 2 lady's maids and 8 servants.

The Census, 1871, for the Farm at Kinsale shows John Clay from Flintshire, who farmed 320 acres with 5 men and 2 boys. Mary, his wife, their son Thomas and daughters Fannie, Helen and Emily. They had five servants.[179] By 1901 daughter

Helen Wright Spinster was now head of the household and her sister Louisa Swann a widow was living there with a nephew Charles Alington and 11 servants and staff.[180]

Jack's children

Harriet Emma Charlotte Mytton (1819–1885) daughter of Jack and Harriet Emma Jones got married on 26 June 1841 to Clement Delves Hill, the fifth son of Colonel John Hill of Hawkstone he had been a captain in the Royal Horse Guards.

Barbara Augusta Mytton the only daughter of Jack and Caroline Mallet Giffard married in 1847 Colonel Poulet George Henry Somerset, MP for twelve years in 1859-71.

John Fox Fitz Giffard Mytton (1823-1875) was born of Jack and Caroline; he was the only one of their five children to pass the age of fifty. He married Martha Gardener and they had five sons. John Gardener Mytton of London; Charles Mytton a Captain in the Merchant Service; Henry Francis Mytton of Winnipeg, Canada; David Christopher Mytton of Cairns, N Queensland and Robert Mytton of Chicago.

John Fox Fitz Gifford Mytton inherited many paternal traits; he sold Habberley in 1846 and Halston having managed to remove the entail on the property the following year. He was ensign in the 53rd Regiment; Lieutenant in the 89th Regiment; Cornet in the Shrops Yeomanry; he retired in 1854 Captain in Kings Own Staffordshire Militia. Resigned in February 1866 and Died 7 February 1875.

Halston Chapel, Halston Hall and Park

The listing of buildings was introduced during World War II to determine which buildings should be rebuilt if they were damaged by bombing. Since then, various planning and protection legislation has been introduced.

Halston is listed as Grade 1 and is now in the care of Rupert and Harriet Harvey. It is a special wedding venue with its own chapel and also operates as a sporting estate, with well-established pheasant, duck and partridge syndicate shoots. There are two lakes, the Big Wood Lake has an area of eighteen acres and the House Lake extends to six acres.[181]

32. Halston Chapel   Author`s Photograph

Halston Chapel

It is called in ancient deeds *Haly-stone* or *Holy-stone*. In the Saxon era the Lordship of Halston belonged to Edric, at which time it was occupied by two Welshmen and one Frenchman. After the Conquest Halston became the property of the Earl of Arundel, or of Robert, Earl of Shrewsbury, and was afterwards bestowed on the Knights of St John of Jerusalem.[182]

In the 26th year of Henry VIII the commandry was valued at £160/14s/ 10d. a year. On the abolition of many of the military-religious orders and monasteries, Henry empowered John Sewster, Esq, Scutifer, and afterwards allowed him to dispose of this manor to Alan Horde, who later exchanged it with Mytton. The alienation was subsequently confirmed by Queen Elizabeth.

33 Halston Chapel Interior   Author`s Photograph

Halston Hall and Park

A mid to late 18th century park around Halston Hall (PRN 00871). Copyright Historic England and used with permission and reproduced in full.[183]

Country house. Circa 1690 with alterations by Robert Mylne for John Mytton 1766-68; further early to mid-C19 additions and alterations.

Red brick with chamfered stone angle quoins and moulded plinth; double-span slate roof with coped verges and eaves parapet with ball finials to corners, including to those of central block.
2 storeys and attic with continuous stone floor band and moulded modillioned eaves cornice with elaborately carved brackets carried up around central pediment; cellars. 2:5:2 bays, centre section forming pedimented break with roundel in moulded stone surround to centre of pediment; glazing bar sashes (15-paned to ground floor) with gauged heads and plain moulded stone cills, including to 'dummy' window to lower right of pedimented section.
Segmental shaped dormers with glazing bar sashes in bottom of roof slope, probably late C18 or C19, one to each side of pediment and 2 to flanking wings. Central entrance; probably early C18 porch with alternating bands of rustication, groove d lintel with projecting keystone, segmental wooden pediment with cartouche and 8-paned glazing bar sashes to sides, approached by flight of 4 steps.
Moulded wooden door surround has 6-panel door with wreathed and radiating lead fanlight set in larger rectangular overlight.
Lead downpipes in angles between pediment and flanking ranges.
Red brick ridge stacks immediately in front of ridge to left and right of pediment have 3 attached and rebated shafts with

moulded stone capping; similar stacks immediately in front of ridge to rear and valley stack to centre. Integral end s tacks with 7 attached and rebated shafts with moulded stone capping over recessed blind round-headed arch, which carries the flues to either side.

Original arrangement to left gable end partly obscured by later addition but right gable end has lunette window to attic over 2 sash windows with gauged heads to first floor. Flanking screen walls to left and right said to be c.1850. Red brick with stone dressings. Semi-circular with 11 blind round headed arches divided by plain pilasters supporting moulded entablature; single-bay projections to ends and buttressed to rear. Garden front.

2 storeys and attic with same details as entrance front bays, outer bays projecting and centre section forming slightly projecting break. Glazing bar sashes (8-paned to ground floor) with gauged heads. The Eaves parapet was rebuilt to original design in 1985. Balustrade in s pace between projecting wings, approached by flight of 6 steps to centre has rather stumpy turned balusters. Lower 5-bay service range slightly set back to right has glazing bar sashes with gauged heads on each floor.

Entrance through mid-C19 stone porch to left with round-headed outer arch and plain entablature over contemporary half-glazed inner door with blind semi-circular fanlight.

Double-span slate roof with tall integral end stack to right and similar stack roughly to centre of rear ridge. Lower rectangular range slightly projecting to right is also early C19 and has low-pitched hipped slate roof, partly concealed by coped parapet. 3 glazing bar sashes with gauged heads to right wall and integral stack with wooden octagonal louvred lantern behind to left corner.

Interior. Entrance hall has stone-flagged floor and raised and fielded panelling to walls. Stone fireplace with fluted consoles. Plaster ceiling with Gothic bosses and leaf decoration to cornice looks Victorian. Double panelled doors in pilastered doorcase to back wall leads to saloon. This is by Mylne with shallow bows at each end and a fine door surround. Ornamental raised and fielded panelling with delicate frieze and cornice. Pedimented glass-fronted wall cupboard to left wall and Adam style marble fireplaces in the centre of each bow. Concealed door to room to left. Room to right of entrance hall is panelled and has built-in wall cupboard with round-headed arch and fluted pilasters. Marble fireplace with late C18 cast-iron hourglass grate. Room to left of saloon has complete raised and fielded panelling with cornice and C18 moulded marble fireplace.

Open-well staircase behind room to right of entrance hall has sturdy turned balusters, plain newel posts and closed string: said to have been brought from a house in Herefordshire. Gothic-style plaster ribbed ceiling above looks Victorian. Several first-floor rooms have raised and fielded panelling with moulded wooden cornices. Moulded wooden fireplaces, some with late C18 cast-iron grates, including several of hour-glass type. Panelled doors throughout. Attic rooms, formerly servants' quarters, have rooms with cast-iron Victorian grates and sets of bells in corridor. One room has reused square oak panelling including to roof slope; several inset panelled wall cupboards with H-hinges Leach gives a photograph of the house and a description. Built in 1690. Alterations of 1776-7 were by Robert Mylne. Edmund Wright, a Manchester merchant, bought the estate and employed Alexander W. Mills of Manchester to make alterations in 1848-9. In 1926-9, Captain and Mrs Joseph Eccles employed Amyas Philips of Hitchin to redecorate much of the interior. The entrance front faces N. It is two-storied, of 9 bays, the central 5 advanced a little under a wide triangular pediment with central oculus. The walling is of fine red brick, with ashlar angle quoins and storey-band, characteristic of the county at the end of C17.

The pediment, if it is of 1690, is the Halston Hall, Ellesmere Road, Halston Site Name Monument Description COUNTRY HOUSE (17th century to Mid-19th century - 1690 AD to 1879 AD).
Evidence EXTANT BUILDING Contact her@shropshire.gov.uk for any queries Page 1 HER Number 00871 Site Name Halston Hall, Ellesmere Road, Halston earliest fully architectural pediment in the county.

Its form, however, with a plain modillion cornice and plain brick parapet, is typical of Mylne. The timber modillion cornice and plain brick parapet are documented as by Mylne, and the sash windows with their thin glazing bars are his too. The steep, gable-ended roof, the over-tall brick chimneystacks and the segment-headed dormer windows peeping over the parapet may all be mid-C19. That is certainly the date of the one-storeyed columned porch, though modified with an outer doorcase of timber added in 1960. The façade was in 1848-9 framed with generous quadrant brick walls with an applied stone Doric order and blind arcading. The E quadrant goes some way to hide the utilitarian service range projecting lopsidedly. Photographed in aerial survey in 2007. Photographed from the air by Chris Musson in 1992. The saloon, alleged to be by Robert Mylne, is such a surprisingly pre-Adam piece of Adamesque that it must make the student uneasy; and with good cause, for documents show it to be the product of the 1920s. But few would suspect, in the absence of documents, that the staircase and the panelling in the dining room, which fit their positions perfectly and appear to be splendid examples of their period, are also of the 1920s. The entrance hall originally corresponded in length with the saloon which it led into: in 1849 the new owners lopped a bay off each end of the hall to contrive two small extra rooms, part of the alterations which made the house 'more convenient. Ground plan. Halston Hall (nameplate confirms), a large country residence now a farmhouse, Mr. Harvey, the farmer/occupier, stated that documents held at the

County Archives Dept., show the house to have been built in 1690. The house is as described above and in good condition.

It can now be seen that the work on the house by Mylne formed part of a general programme of improvement touching on all aspects of the estate put in hand by John Mytton 2 (d. 1783). That was in progress by the earlier 1770s and presumably followed his return from the Grand Tour and his marriage to Rebecca Pigot of Chetwynd.

A map of 1765 (Shrews. Local Studies Libr. Plan 66) may be preparatory to the campaign. That hints at a formal layout west of the house, presumably contemporary with the house of c. 1690, with a pair of small, square buildings (? Garden-end summerhouses) and a squat, rectangular pond. Other ponds lay north-east of the Hall. Presumably these were mainly for fish, although the largest, with a very angular plan, may have been the 'triangular pool' mentioned by Mytton on the 1770s as 'formerly a turbary, great part of which was burnt and afterwards made into a pool about the year 1742' (Shrews. Local Studies Libr., Deeds 13192). 'Lawns' lay north of the house, extending to the main road, and south of the house running down to the river Perry.

The most striking element of the landscape in 1765, however, was a half-mile long ride running east from the house for the full length of the woodland called 'the Park' (the modern Big Wood), off which at angles ran shorter, supplementary rides. In the 1770s, when John Mytton wrote detailed memoranda on the management of the Halston estate, the edges of the paths were being planted up with evergreens; Mytton mentions hollies and laurel but not rhododendrons, still to be seen in Big Wood in 1995, which may therefore be a later introduction. Unless the squirrels were destroyed Mytton thought it highly inadvisable to plant 'any kind of fir, as they are particularly fond of the young buds of a pine.' Along the south, garden, front of the house was a kidney-shaped? Shrubbery, with winding paths. That may have been very new in 1765, and may already have been defined to the south by the ha-ha present in 1995. Presumably these elements comprised the 'walks and pleasure grounds' mentioned by Mytton in the 1770s. Was his the 'old lawn' noted by Mytton as appearing to have been built up by soil perhaps cast out of the foundation of the house when it was originally built? (Shrews. Local Studies Libr., Deeds 13192). They and kitchen gardens, occupied a gardener, four men, and two women. The grass along the sides of the woodland paths was mowed three times a year that of the main shrubbery and gardens more regularly as required, and as far as was practicable between 6 and 8 a.m. (Shrops. R.O. 398/1, pp. 177-8, 187-8; for the gardener's duties see also Shrews. Local Studies Libr., Deeds 13667, pp. 118-20). The shrubbery and the Park were connected by a path carried under the track or drive to Halston chapel. The arched bridge was still extant in 1995, although the path from the former shrubbery stopped at that point.

A campaign of improvement to the grounds of Halston probably began at about the same time, in 1771, that Richard Handley, a Newport man, was engaged as gardener at 16 guineas a year in place of his long-time predecessor James Phillips (Shrews. Local Studies Libr., Deeds 13667, p. 16). By the time (c. 1777) Mytton wrote his memoranda books, presumably for the guidance of his young son John (d. 1798: Shrops. A.O., Halston catalogue), and since the estate was mapped in 1765 (above), the main feature of the park had been laid out, a serpentine lake almost a mile long. As yet, it is not clear who was responsible for this. William Emes certainly visited here (inf. From Mr. J.B. Lawson), while in 1775 a drawing for the east half of the lake (there called the 'new river'), showing a layout very similar to that actually executed, was done by T. Slater (Shrews. Local Studies Libr., Deeds 19530; ref. owed to Mr. Lawson). The new lake (called the Great Pool in the later 18th century: Shrews. Local Studies Libr., Deeds 136 9), running south of the park and the house, represented an enlargement of a length of the river Perry, the first 150m of which, at the west end, was canalized. At that point, where it was crossed by a bridge carrying the path from the Hall to the kitchen garden, a rusticated cascade was constructed with a mid-stream island, planted about with yews. Towards the east end of the Pool was the Great Island (Shrews. Local Studies Libr., Deeds 13679). A detailed memorandum by John Mytton (Shrews. Local Studies Libr., Deeds 13192, pp. [4-5, 24-6] reveals that the lake was in fact dug in two separate campaigns, with excavation of the west half beginning in June 1773 and continuing until 1775, while the east end, including the Great Island, was constructed between April 1777 and July 1778. In all Mytton reckoned the cost to have been about 1::530.

Midway along the lake, below the house, was a bridge which gave access to the timber framed Halston chapel (Listed Grade I: 1582/11/127)100m beyond, which formed a picturesque eye catcher from the Hall. By 1765 the chapel stood in complete isolation, but in 1995 it was clear from extensive earthworks, including hollow ways, spreading east and west of it on its south side, that it had once stood towards the centre of a hamlet. Whether this was deliberately removed by the Myttons at some stage between 1690 and 1765, or whether desertion had fortuitously occurred anyway, is unknown. Already in 1765, the bridge had apparently been made picturesque - the map of that date hints at a Chinese style - and this was changed further in the following years. In 1769 Mylne designed a wooden bridge, but this design was altered in 1778, the year the Great Pool was completed, to a 'wooden bridge on ropes', perhaps a mock suspension bridge (C. Gotch, 'A Shropshire Vogue. Notes and correspondence Relating to Robert Mylne' (Typescript, copy in Shrew. Local Studies Libr., classmark C71vf). It is unknown whether either of those two bridges was constructed although by c.1780 there were two bridges towards the centre of the Pool (Shrews. Local Studies Libr., Deeds 13192, p. [24]. Also unknown is whether any of Mylne's other proposals of the 1770s were carried out. These included converting, or concealing, an existing pigeon house as a 'Doric Temple', constructing 'an ice well and a stable over it', and adding a spire to the tower of the church (Shrews. Local Studies Libr., MS. 2498, 20 May 1784; Gotch, op. cit). There is an icehouse (Listed Grade II: 1582/11/126), west of the house and in the vicinity of one of the 1765 summerhouses, but this (an apsidal-ended building), although a later 18th-century building, is concealed beneath a tree covered mound rather than stables.

Also, of 1765 x c.1777, and probably 1772 when a new garden wall was built (Shrews. Local Studies Libr., Deeds 13192, p. [4]), are the kitchen gardens, which lie 500 m west of the Hall, on the main road from Oswestry to Ellesmere. The wisdom of placing them here was already much in doubt in 1777, but 'the error was discovered too late to be remediable'. The' position, Mytton noted, lay them open to 'evil' - presumably the theft of produce - while their distance from the house made it difficult for a single gardener to superintend efficiently both the kitchen gardens and the pleasure grounds (Shrops. R.O. 398/1, pp. 177-8). Much of the fabric of the walls of the 5-acre gardens is of c. 1770, including the two-storey cottage on the north-east corner and the range of potting sheds along the outside of the north wall. Other fabric, including ornamental ball finials on south and west entrances (a third entrance, on the north, is plain), presumably dates from c. 1851, when it was reported that vineries and greenhouses were under construction (S. Bagshaw, Directory of Shropshire (1851), 147-8). Also, of that date may be the stone wall screening the garden from the road. The brick garden walls, sheds and cottage are all Listed Grade II: 1582/11/128.

The final elements of improvements to the surrounds of Halston in the 1770s that can be suggested is the planting of clumps of specimen trees in the park, and the opening up of the shrubbery south of the Hall to give an improved view; perhaps associated with the latter was the construction of the shrubbery wall in 1778 (Shrews. Local Studies Libr., Deeds 13192, p. [4]; see also the view of Halston published in 1796: Shrews. Local Studies Lbr., Waton's Press Cuttings, vol. 2, p. 501 a). 'Flowers' were purchase from Christopher Whittingham, presumably one of the well-known Coventry nurseryman family of that name (Shrews. Local Studies Libr., MS. 2498, 2 Oct. 1784; J. Harvey, Early Nurserymen (1974), 94-5). Estate memoranda record the purchase of large numbers of trees - Black spruce, Scotch Fir, beeches, witch elms, Horse chestnuts, and sycamores (Shrews. Local Studies Libr., Deeds 13192, p. [11] - as well as their production in the Halston nursery (shown on the 1765 plan as within the later New Park). Some 200 north-west of the Hall is an artificial low mound on top of which are the stumps of several large trees sawn down several years before 1995; although the condition of the top of the stump was poor it was still possible to count, fairly accurately, c. 200 rings. The clump was not mapped in 1765.

Although his role is unknown it seems likely that day to day oversight of the improvements to the estate in the 1770s was the responsibility of Alexander Maccattie, Mytton's 'Surveyor of Works' or 'Overseer of Ground Works', to whom he left E20 in a codicil added to his will in 1778 (Shrops. R.O. 2313/138), a sum finally paid in November 1784. He remained in the employ of Halston until at least the end of the same year, at a salary of 35 guineas a year (Shrews. Local Studies Libr., MS. 2498). One would like to know more of Maccattie, who was clearly well off in his own right, sufficient at any rate to lend Mytton £250 (Shrews. Local Studies Libr., MS. 2498).

By the end of the 18th century the park had begun to creep south of the Pool, although by then only 10 acres were so inclosed (Shrews. Local Studies Libr., Deeds 13679). By 1827 'New Park', as the parkland south of the Pool was termed, was much larger than the imparked area to the north. The south border of New Park was planted up with a broad shelter belt flanking a ride or walk (C. and J. Greenwood, Map of Shropshire (1827)). The shelter belt flanked the new course of the river Perry, which was much improved and straightened by Act and Award of 1777 and 1783 (report by P.A. Stamper for English Heritage North-West Wetlands Survey). In 1995 New Park was under arable cultivation; some parkland trees survived, notably a clump on an artificial mound south of the main island in the lake.

The major alterations of c. 1850 to the Hall and kitchen gardens have already been noted. Also of that date may be the main gateway to Halston, a surprisingly modest affair of iron gates flanked by low, curving stone walls, probably a remodelling of the entrance shown on the 1765 plan. It was perhaps also then that the immediate surrounds of the Hall were modified, with the removal of the large pond north-east of the Hall (called Blacksmith's pool in 1847: Shrops. R.O. 2171/138). Then, or perhaps nearer the end of the 19th century, topiarised yew bushes were planted along the south front of the Hall. The heronry, a notable feature in 1995 of the north side of the lake, was mentioned in 1901 (S. Leighton, Shropshire Houses, (1901), 26).

Photographed during aerial survey 2007-2008. A parkland plan was undertaken in July 2013 of part of the historic parkland at Halston Hall, which is subject to a Higher-level Stewardship Agreement. This included a history of the park, an overview of survival of the park, statement of significance and parkland tree planting plan. Stamper argues that the major alterations to the Hall of c. 1850 may have been accompanied by more modest changes to the park. These are likely to have involved the remodelling of the gateway at the top of the main drive and perhaps also to the immediate environs of the hall, including the removal of the ponds north-west of the house which are shown on a 1765 plan and changes to the western end of the ha-ha.

Subsequently the park remained largely unchanged across the course of the later 19th century.
In World War II the park (but not the hall) was requisitioned and a US military hospital (1,084 beds) established [see PRN 28471].

Just under the ground surface there remains part of U.S. Army Hospital Center 804 a WWII United States Military Hospital comprising over 100 buildings, in the grounds of Halston Park to the north of Halston Hall. Only one roofed building survives. The cropmark remains of individual buildings are visible on vertical aerial photography, and possible represents below ground remains of concrete bases and floors of buildings. It is likely that the construction of the hospital resulted in the felling of some parkland trees, adjacent to the main drive and north of the hall. Halston Hall was one of the five U.S. military hospital sites in the Shropshire/Flintshire area during World War II. The headquarters of this cluster was originally located in Gwernheylod, Flintshire but was later moved to Whitchurch, Shropshire.[184]

Mytton Miscellany

Thomas Mytton (by 1344), became a very successful wool merchant and is listed on the guild merchant roll by 1344.[185] He was one of many merchants who lent money to the crown in the 1350s. Thomas is shown as bailiff in 1360 on a pedigree chart held in Shropshire Archives.[186] His son Reginald was also trading in wool and was a leading exporter through the port of London.[187]

Richard Mytton has signed a lease on a tenement in Frankwell as Master of the Shrewsbury Drapers on the document dated 1 February 1519.[188]

John Mytton? – 1550 A member of the Shrewsbury Drapers Company, this Mytton did not have the ambition and drive of some of his kin and was described as an exception to the very exploitative nature of Drapers generally. On his death in 1550 a commentator said he was a `*true occupier who dealt justly with all those shearmen that wrought[189] for him; he never stopped with them any penny but paid them always in ready money*`[190]

John Mytton iii is listed as a subscriber of Phillips T. *The History and Antiquities of Shrewsbury from its first Foundation to the present Time* (Shrewsbury, 1779)[191]
He also sold the land upon which the Shrewsbury Flax Mill was built by Bage in 1797and built houses for the artisans.[192]

Richard Mytton 1751 -1828 inherited an estate at Garth near Guilsfield and was loaned on mortgage £25,000 by Dr Robert Darwin to build Garth Hall the loan interest rate was 4.5% per annum.[193]

Edward Mytton of Shipton appears in Shropshire in 1615 from Worcester.[194] Later Henry Mytton became bailiff of the Wenlock liberty.

34. The Mytton Arms Habberley   Author`s Photograph

Recorded as The Forge in 1825 and operated by Richard Lewis a blacksmith. The name was changed to the Mytton Arms in 1840 when Ann Beddows ran the business. Kate Mackenzie is the present innkeeper and she arranged for me to meet local historian Muriel Lewis who supplied the details of the name and date changes.[195]

Mytton Antiques
An antique shop on the old A5 near Attingham Park, where prior to the building of the present Attingham Hall it was two estate cottages.

Mytton and Mermaid
An historic hotel next to Atcham Bridge named after the Mytton family and a legendary mermaid.

The Jack Mytton Way

The Jack Mytton Way travels through nearly 100 miles of Shropshire's most beautiful and unspoilt countryside. Rural byways, bridleways and quiet country lanes lead you through Shropshire's historic market towns and sleepy villages, across open moorland and past ancient earthworks. The southern loop, over secluded parts of the Shropshire Hills, means that you can now do a circular ride. Open to horse riders, cyclists and walkers the majority of the route is off road.[196]

The Mytton Inn Nr Whittington?
Presently closed and undergoing refurbishment (Nov 2018)[197]

Why is it called Mytton Oak Remembrance Park?
The name was chosen following a public consultation in which people were invited to put forward their suggestions. The choice of name recognises the location of the new park just off Mytton Oak Road, which took its name, in 1934, from the fact that land in the area once belonged to the Mytton family.
To recognise the origins of the park's chosen name, we plan to plant at the site an oak tree which descends from the Shelton Oak – a tree which for more than 600 years stood close to the park site on the land once owned by the Mytton family – and from which the name Mytton Oak is thought to originate. Though the Shelton Oak died in the 1940s, documents show that in the 1880s an oak tree, grown from one of its acorns, was planted in the Dingle in The Quarry.
Now, the plan is to take an acorn from the tree in the Dingle and use it to grow an oak tree at the new park, providing a link back to the original tree.

Bicton Heath Racecourse

Racecourse Lane in Bicton is a clue to the location of the old racecourse on land owned by the Mytton family on Bicton Heath. It was used from 1724 to 1832, but the land had to be sold in 1834 for the benefit of Mad Jacks Mytton`s creditors. The circuit finished in Pump Lane near the grandstand close to The Grapes known a cock-fighting inn. Jack Mytton was said to have stayed in Bowbrook House.

The racecourse was relocated to Monkmoor Road in 1832 and racing became successful there under the management of John Frail who took over in 1843. Racing continued until shortly after he was elected as mayor in 1878 as he died in office the following year. The Council bought the land in Monkmoor for housing for £3,500 in 1925.[198]

Mytton in the US

Many members of the family emigrated to the US, where Jack was celebrated by the Jack Mytton Run, an annual streaking event by students of the University of Minnesota. Participants ran across Northrup Mall on the first day of the new term following spring break. It is reported to have begun in 1999 and continued until 2009 when it was ended by campus police.

End Notes & References

[1] Notes are taken from the edition published by Philamore in 1986

[2] Morris J., *Domesday Book, Shropshire*. Edited by Thorn F & Thorn C. (Chichester, 1986) Notes 3d.5.

[3] in *The Cartulary of Haughmond Abbey*, ed Una Rees (Cardiff, 1985)

[4] Gelling M., in collaboration with H D G Foxall, *The Placenames of Shropshire - Part One* (English Place-Name Society, 1990) p. 217.

[5] Thornycroft D., *In Direct Descent* (Published, 2003) p.4.

[6] Powys Land Club, Montgomery Collections. *Myttons of Garth- Pedigree. 1890.* Extracts from the article provided by Neil Mytton July 2021

[7] Thornycroft D., *In Direct Descent* (Published, 2003) p.4.

[8] Blakeway *Sheriffs of Shropshire* (Shrewsbury, 1831) p.77-79.

[9] VCH Shropshire. Thacker A.T., Cromarty D., contributions by Champion W.A., and Cromarty R. in *A History of Shropshire Vol VI, Part 1.* (London, 2014) p. 58.

[10] Powys Land Club, Montgomery Collections. *Myttons of Garth-Pedigree. 1890.* Extracts from the article provided by Neil Mytton July 2021

[11] Thornycroft D., *In Direct Descent* (Published, 2003) p.5.

[12] VCH Shropshire. Thacker A.T., Cromarty D., contributions by Champion W.A., in *A History of Shropshire Vol VI, Part 1.* (London, 2014) p.106.

[13] VCH Shropshire. Thacker A.T., Cromarty D., contributions by Champion W.A., and Cromarty R. in *A History of Shropshire Vol VI, Part 1.* (London, 2014) p. 106.

[14] Cromarty D and R, *The Wealth of Shrewsbury in the Early Fourteenth Century* (Shrewsbury 1993) p.63 Forinseci were new traders who paid higher fees than the existing merchants to start trading in Shrewsbury.

[15] Thornycroft D., *In Direct Descent* (Published, 2003) p.5. The Pride`s were another wealthy dynasty of Shrewsbury traders and owned much property in town so much that their name was given to Pride Hill.

[16] Leighton W.A. *Early Chronicles of Shrewsbury transcribed and annotated from Dr Taylor`s manuscript.* Transactions May 1880 p.239.

[17] SA.6000/3678.

[18] SA.3365/448,3.

[19] Baker N., *Shrewsbury An Archaeological Assessment of an English Border Town* (Oxford 2010) p. 174.

[20] Baker N., *Shrewsbury An Archaeological Assessment of an English Border Town* (Oxford 2010) p. 175.

[21] Moran M. *Vernacular Buildings of Shropshire* (Almerley, 2003) p.237.

[22] Leighton S. *Mytton Manuscripts* in Powys Land Club 1875 Collections Historical & Archaeological relating to Montgomeryshire Volume Viii p308

[23] Powys Land Club, Montgomery Collections. *Myttons of Garth- Pedigree. 1890.* Extracts from the article provided by Neil Mytton July 2021.

[24] Leighton W.A. *Early Chronicles of Shrewsbury transcribed and annotated from Dr Taylor`s manuscript.* Transactions May 1880, p239.

[25] VCH Shropshire. Thacker A.T., Cromarty D., contributions by Champion W.A., and Cromarty R. in *A History of Shropshire Vol VI, Part 1.* (London, 2014) p. 90.

[26] Nimrod. *Life of Mytton* (London,1837) p.2.

[27] Leighton S. Mytton Manuscripts in Powis Land Club 1875

[28] Nimrod. *Life of Mytton* (London,1837) p.2.

[29] Jackson M *Castles of Shropshire* (Carlisle 1988) p 14-16.

[30] VCH Shropshire. Thacker A.T., Cromarty D., contributions by Champion W.A., Cromarty R. in *A History of Shropshire Vol VI, Part 1.* (London, 2014) p .94.

[31] Coulton B. *Regime & Religion Shrewsbury 1400-1700* (Almeley, 2010) p.26.

[32] Thornycroft D., *In Direct Descent* (Published, 2003) p. 11.

[33] Leighton S. *Mytton Manuscripts* in Powys Land Club 1875 Collections Historical & Archaeological relating to Montgomeryshire Volume Viii p309.

[34] Forrest H.E. *The Old Houses of Shrewsbury* p.90.

[35] Nimrod. *Life of Mytton* (London, 1837) p. 2.

[36] Transactions Series 3 Vol1 p.170.

[37] http://www.historyofparliamentonline.org/volume/1509-1558/member/mytton-adam-1498-1561 Accessed 21/05/2021

[38] Mendenhall T.C., *The Shrewsbury Drapers and the Welsh Wool Trade in the XVI and XVII Centuries* (Oxford, 1953) p.135. Knyvet was commissioner appointed to search for lands that should have passed to the crown under the 1547 statute. He claimed the Shrewsbury Drapers were maintaining a priest.

[39] Thomas Cromwell would do anything to advance himself and Henry VIII

[40] http://www.historyofparliamentonline.org/volume/1509-1558/member/mytton-adam-1498-1561 Accessed 21/05/2021 .

[41] Moran, M. *Vernacular Buildings of Shropshire* (Almeley,2003) p.249.

[42] Cromarty R. *Trans. Salop Arch. Soc.* Vol LXXV 2000, p15-48.

[43] Moran, M. *Vernacular Buildings of Shropshire* (Almeley,2003) p.250.

[44] *It is from the History of Parliament, Volumes: 1509-1558.Written by D. F. Coros that is the source of much information.*

[45] SA. 3766/2/2/4. Pedigree Chart of Mytton family on paper.

[46] Powys Land Club, Montgomery Collections. *Myttons of Garth- Pedigree. 1890.* Extracts from the article provided by Neil Mytton July 2021

[47] Thornycroft D., *In Direct Descent* (Published, 2003) p. 11.

[48] Shrewsbury Guildhall 66, unnumbered; *Trans. Salop Arch. Soc.* (ser. 4), xii. 184-5; *LP Hen. VIII*, xviii; Req.2/197/12.

[49] VCH Shropshire. Thacker A.T., Cromarty D., contributions by Champion W.A., and Cromarty R. in *A History of Shropshire Vol VI, Part 1.* (London, 2014) p. 90.

[50] Coulton B. *Regime & Religion Shrewsbury 1400-1700* (Almeley, 2010) p.40.

[51] http://www.historyofparliamentonline.org/volume/1509-1558/member/mytton-richard-15001-91 Accessed 31/05/2021

[52] https://www.british-history.ac.uk/vch/salop/vol2/pp87-88#p8

[53] https://biography.wales/article/s-FITZ-ALA1135 Accessed 4/03/2021

[54] The most prominent members in the Commons were the knights of the shire. During the Middle Ages two knights were elected for each of the 37 counties under royal jurisdiction. In 1536 the twelve counties of Wales were incorporated into English rule by statute and they gained the right to return one member each to Parliament. Later two counties long seen as outside royal jurisdiction, the county palatines of Chester and Durham, were also able to return two members each to Parliament, from 1543 and 1673 respectively. When a new Parliament was summoned, writs were issued from Chancery (the royal secretariat) to the county's sheriff to call a County Court for an election of knights of the shire, and in the early days of Parliament all freemen, that is those who were not serfs, had the right to vote for their representatives.
https://www.parliament.uk/about/livingheritage/evolutionofparliament/origi nsofparliament/birthofparliament/overview/knights/

[55] *Trans. Salop Arch. Soc.* (ser. 3), ii, 145 seq.; Holinshed, *Chron.* iv. 14; D. M. Loades, *Two Tudor Conspiracies*, 96; C3/49/62; Req.2/197/12.

[56] Marian Parliaments were shortly after the time of the death of Mary, when many exiles returned to England and their political careers..

[57] Torin L., The history of the Corps of the King's Shropshire Light Infantry, Vol IV, (Shrewsbury, 1987) p.112.

[58] PCC 3 Sheffielde; *Trans. Salop Arch. Soc.* (ser. 3), ii. 149; Blakeway, *Salop Sheriffs*, 87; *Lichfield Wills and Admin. 1516-1652* (Index Lib. vii), 284.

[59] Thornycroft D., *In Direct Descent* (Published, 2003) p. 11.

[60] An escheator supervised the reversion of property of a deceased person, who died without an heir, to the state.

[61] Shrewsbury Guildhall 76, f. 22v; 486, f. 71. Author's: P. S. Edwards History of Parliament

[62] Leighton S. *Mytton Manuscripts* in Powys Land Club 1875 Collections Historical & Archaeological relating to Montgomeryshire Volume Viii p309.

[63] Transactions VOL XLVII 1933-34 P.97.

[64] Mendenhall T.C., *The Shrewsbury Drapers and the Welsh Wool Trade in the XVI and XVII Centuries* (Oxford, 1953) p.51.

[65] Mendenhall T.C., *The Shrewsbury Drapers and the Welsh Wool Trade in the XVI and XVII Centuries* (Oxford, 1953) p.64.

[66] Thornycroft D., *In Direct Descent* (Published, 2003) p. 12.

[67] Transactions VOL XLVII 1933-34 P.98.

[68] Worton J. *To Settle the Crown, Waging Civil War in Shropshire1642-1648.* (Solihull–2016) p xxiii.

[69] Bracher T. & Emmett R., *Shropshire in the Civil War* (Shrewsbury, 2000) p 23.

[70] Bracher T. & Emmett R., *Shropshire in the Civil War* (Shrewsbury, 2000) p 91.

[71] Bracher T. & Emmett R., *Shropshire in the Civil War* (Shrewsbury, 2000) p 23.

[72] Worton J., *To Settle the Crown, Waging Civil War in Shropshire1642-1648.* (Solihull, 2016) p. xxv.

[73] Worton J., *To Settle the Crown, Waging Civil War in Shropshire1642-1648.* (Solihull, 2016) p. 85.

[74] Worton J. *To Settle the Crown, Waging Civil War in Shropshire1642-1648.* (Solihull, 2016) p 118.

[75] Sir Thomas Myddleton, was the sergeant-major-general and commander in chief of the six shires.

[76] Coulton B. *Regime & Religion Shrewsbury 1400-1700* (Almely, 2010) p. 98.

[77] Bracher T. & Emmett R., *Shropshire in the Civil War* (Shrewsbury. 2000) p 38.

[78] Worton J. *To Settle the Crown, Waging Civil War in Shropshire1642-1648.* (Solihull, 2016) p 121.

[79] Worton J. *To Settle the Crown, Waging Civil War in Shropshire1642-1648.* (Solihull, 2016) p. 96.

[80] Worton J. *To Settle the Crown, Waging Civil War in Shropshire 1642 -1648* (Solihull,2016) p.82-99.

[81] Bracher T.& Emmett R., *Shropshire in the Civil War* (Shrewsbury, 2000) p 72.

[82] Worton J. *To Settle the Crown, Waging Civil War in Shropshire1642-1648.* (Solihull, 2016) p 122.

[83] Worton J. *To Settle the Crown, Waging Civil War in Shropshire1642-1648.* (Solihull, 2016) p 123.

[84] Worton J. *To Settle the Crown, Waging Civil War in Shropshire1642-1648*. (Solihull, 2016) p 122.

[85] Worton J. *To Settle the Crown, Waging Civil War in Shropshire1642-1648*. (Solihull, 2016) p 105.

[86] Worton J. *To Settle the Crown, Waging Civil War in Shropshire 1642 -1648* (Solihull, 2016) p.180.

[87] Worton J. *To Settle the Crown, Waging Civil War in Shropshire 1642 -1648* (Solihull, 2016) p.188.

[88] Worton J. *To Settle the Crown, Waging Civil War in Shropshire 1642 -1648* (Solihull, 2016) p.228.

[89] Worton J. *To Settle the Crown, Waging Civil War in Shropshire 1642 -1648* (Solihull, 2016) p.227.

[90] Worton J. *To Settle the Crown, Waging Civil War in Shropshire 1642 -1648* (Solihull, 2016) p.155.

[91] Auden J.E. *My Case with the Committee of Salop – Colonel Mytton versus the Parliamentary Committee.* Transactions of the Shropshire Archaeological Society Volume XLVIII 1934-1935 p 49-60.

[92] He was London based and a member of the Merchant Adventurers' Co. c.1607; and also a member of the Drapers' Co. 1623, master 1642-3.

[93] https://historyofparliamentonline.org/volume/1604-1629/member/mytton-henry-1651 Accessed 4/2/21

[94] Thornycroft D., *In Direct Descent* (Published, 2003) p. 15.

[95] Transactions VOL XLVII 1933-34 P.98

[96] http://www.historyofparliamentonline.org/volume/1690-1715/member/mytton-richard-1660-1718 Accessed 31/05/2021

[97] http://www.historyofparliamentonline.org/volume/1690-1715/member/mytton-richard-1660-1718 Accessed 31/05/2021

[98] Leighton S. *Mytton Manuscripts* in Powys Land Club 1875 Collections Historical & Archaeological relating to Montgomeryshire Volume Viii p.309.

[99] http://www.historyofparliamentonline.org/volume/1690-1715/member/mytton-richard-1660-1718 Accessed 31/05/2021

[100] Leighton S. *Mytton Manuscripts* in Powys Land Club 1875 Collections Historical & Archaeological relating to Montgomeryshire Volume Viii p.309.

[101] Leighton S. *Mytton Manuscripts* in Powys Land Club 1875 Collections Historical & Archaeological relating to Montgomeryshire Volume Viii p.309.

[102] Nimrod., *Life of Mytton* (London,1837) p.3.

[103] https://archiveshub.jisc.ac.uk/search/archives/49e01fa8-6b92-3e1f-ad5d-b046874682fc Accessed 03/02/2021.

[104] Cathrall William, *History of Oswestry* (Oswestry, 1871) p.252.

[105] https://discovery.nationalarchives.gov.uk/details/r/f3a14625-86cb-420c-a6e2-746462fb9aff Accessed 03/02/2021

[106] His marriage to Rebecca Pigot of Chetwynd (settlement 1767: Shrops. R.O. 2313/137).

[107] A map of 1765 (Shrews. Local Studies Libr. Plan 66) may be preparatory to the campaign.

[108] Cathrall William, *History of Oswestry* (Oswestry 1871) p.250.

[109] S.A. 398/1 *Halston Estate Book* John Mytton (Halton About 1770s)

[110] Holdsworth J., *Mango* (London, 1972) p. 17.

[111] Col.Wingfield. *The Shropshire Yeomanry Cavalry 1795-1887*. (Shrewsbury, 1888) Adnitt & Naunton, p. 10.

[112] Col.Wingfield. *The Shropshire Yeomanry Cavalry 1795-1887*. (Shrewsbury, 1888) p. 10.

[113] Col.Wingfield. *The Shropshire Yeomanry Cavalry 1795-1887*. (Shrewsbury, 1888) p. 11.

[114] Col.Wingfield. *The Shropshire Yeomanry Cavalry 1795-1887*. (Shrewsbury, 1888) p. 10.

[115] Col.Wingfield. *The Shropshire Yeomanry Cavalry 1795-1887*. (Shrewsbury, 1888) p. 19.

[116] Col.Wingfield. *The Shropshire Yeomanry Cavalry 1795-1887*. (Shrewsbury, 1888) p. 19.

[117] S.A. 6000/13322. Indenture re Sale of land to build Flax Mill Maltings.

[118] Col.Wingfield. *The Shropshire Yeomanry Cavalry 1795-1887*. (Shrewsbury, 1888) p. 11.

[119] Holdsworth J., *Mango* (London, 1972) p.19-20.

[120] Holdsworth J., *Mango* (London, 1972) p.29.

[121] Holdsworth J., *Mango* (London, 1972) p.34.

[122] Holdsworth J., *Mango* (London, 1972) p. 41.

[123] Memories collected by *The Elizabethan group memories of former pupils*

[124] Holdsworth J., *Mango* (London, 1972) p. 42.

[125] Holdsworth J., *Mango* (London, 1972) p. 43.

[126] Contact with the university established that there is no record of him having attended a lecture at Cambridge.

[127] Holdsworth J., *Mango* (London, 1972) p. 53.

[128] Holdsworth J., *Mango* (London, 1972) p. 45.

[129] Holdsworth J., *Mango* (London, 1972) p. 58.

[130] Holdsworth J., *Mango* (London, 1972) p. 58-60.

[131] Col.Wingfield. *The Shropshire Yeomanry Cavalry 1795-1887*. (Shrewsbury, 1888) Adnitt & Naunton, p. 23.

[132] Col.Wingfield. *The Shropshire Yeomanry Cavalry 1795-1887*. (Shrewsbury, 1888) Adnitt & Naunton, p. 23.

[133] Col.Wingfield. *The Shropshire Yeomanry Cavalry 1795-1887*. (Shrewsbury, 1888) Adnitt & Naunton, p. 44.

[134] Col.Wingfield. *The Shropshire Yeomanry Cavalry 1795-1887*. (Shrewsbury, 1888) Adnitt & Naunton, p. 51.

[135] Stingo was a strong beer matured in Oak casks and usually brewed at least a year in advance.

[136] Local press reports.

[137] Nimrod., *Life of Mytton* (London,1837)

[138] Filberts in a carriage

[139] S A 2313/148-9 Settlement on intended marriage of John Mytton and Harriet Emma Jones.

[140] SA XLSP792 D55.7 Howell T., *Poll Book 1819* (Shrewsbury, 1819).

[141] http://www.historyofparliamentonline.org/volume/1820-1832/member/corbett-panton-1785-1855 Accessed 30/05/2021

[142] SA X655/3/24 Eddowes Gazette 17 May 1819. List of Burgesses voting

[143] Nimrod. *Life of Mytton* (London,1903) p.159.

[144] www.historyofparliamentonline.org/volume/1790-1820/member/mytton-john-1796-1834 Accessed 19/10/2018.

[145] https://www.historyofparliamentonline.org/volume/1820-1832/constituencies/shrewsbury Accessed 02/03/21.

[146] https://www.nationalarchives.gov.uk/currency-converter/#currency-result Accessed 6/03/2021.

[147] Nimrod., *Life of Mytton* (London,1837) p. 43.

[148] Nimrod., *Life of Mytton* (London,1837) p.60.

[149] Staffordshire Advertiser 12 December 1818.

[150] Nimrod., *Life of Mytton* (London,1903) p.165.

[151] Nimrod., *Life of Mytton* (London,1837) p.111.

[152] Nimrod., *Life of Mytton* (London,1903) p.178.

[153] S.A. 2313/155-156 Marriage settlement between John Mytton and Caroline Giffard

[154] Holdsworth J., *Mango* (London 1972) p. 118.

[155] http://oswestry-tc.gov.uk/oswestry-archives/oswestry-town-mayors-from-1674.html Accessed 17/10/2018.

[156] Nimrod. Apperley. *Life of Mytton* (London,1837) p.60.

[157] Nimrod. Apperley. *Life of Mytton* (London,1837) p.61.

[158] Nimrod. Apperley. *The Life of John Mytton, Esq* (London1903) p.114.

[159] VCH Shropshire Vol II p. 194.   Byegones, ii 278; vi. 315

[160] VCH Shropshire Vol II p. 194. Buckley G. B., *New Light on pre-Victorian Cricket* 1937 p.112.

[161] VCH Shropshire Vol II p. 195. Buckley G. B., *New Light on pre-Victorian Cricket* 1937 p.112.

[162] S.A. D3651/B/29/11 25 March 1821 Mortgage Loan by Thomas Parr to John Mytton

[163] S A D3651/D/20/670 Salt collection Draft Conveyance *John Mytton to R W Darwin.*

[164] S.A. D3651/D/20/670 3 Day auction sale of property in and around Shrewsbury.

[165] S.A. Letter from JM to John Mott of the Close, Lichfield.
Acquired by Mr Jack Wilding of Shrewsbury who gave permission for it to be reproduced in the Shropshire Magazine May/June 1952.

[166] Nimrod., *Life of Mytton* (London,1903) p.169.

[167] Nimrod., *Life of Mytton* (London,1903) p.47

[168] Nimrod., *Life of Mytton* (London,1903) p.39.

[169] Nimrod., *Life of Mytton* (London,1837) p. 64.

[170] Nimrod., *Life of Mytton* (London,1903) p.43

[171] Nimrod., *Life of Mytton* (London,1903) p.46.

[172] Nimrod., *Life of Mytton* (London,1837) p.58.

[173] Holdsworth J., *Mango* (London 1972) p.157.

[174] Nimrod., *Life of Mytton* (London,1903) p.81.

[175] Holdsworth J., *Mango* (London 1972) p.159.

[176] Darwell R., *Madcap`s Progress* (London 1938) p. 170.

[177] S A XLE1/1060/7/3/R318631 Poll Book of Salop1831

[178] S A Times report of the death of John Mytton.

[179] 1871 Census accessed 17/03/2021

[180] 1901 Census accessed on line 21 /3/2021

[181] www.halstonestate.co.uk/home_country_house_weddings_shropshire.html# Accessed 18/11/2018

[182] Cathrall William, *History of Oswestry* (Oswestry, 1871) p249.

[183] © Historic England [2021].
The National Heritage List Text Entries contained in this material were obtained on 14/06/2021. The most publicly available up to date National Heritage List Text Entries can be obtained from http://www.historicengland.org.uk/listing/the-list/

[184] Collins M & F. *Hospital 804* Accessed 17/03/2021
http://www.englemed.co.uk/books/usaaf/hospital804.htm

[185] Drinkwater C. H., *Seven Shrewsbury gild merchant rolls of the 14th century,* TSANHS 3rd ser.3 (1903), 66, SA 3365/802. (The roll is the list of merchants that were permitted to ply their trade in Shrewsbury)

[186] SA 3766/2/2/4. Pedigree Chart of Mytton family on paper.

[187] VCH, Shropshire. Thacker A.T., Cromarty D., contributions by Champion W.A., and Cromarty R. in *A History of Shropshire Vol VI, Part 1.* (London, 2014) p.58.

[188] S A 1831/2/8/16 Lease of a tenement in Mardol and a croft in Frankwell

[189] Made or fashioned in the specified way

[190] Mendenhall T.C., *The Shrewsbury Drapers and the Welsh Wool Trade in the XVI and XVII Centuries* (Oxford, 1953) p.45.

[191] Phillips T. *The History and Antiquities of Shrewsbury from its first Foundation to the present Time* (Shrewsbury, 1779) p. 9.

[192] S.A. 6000/13322. Indenture of land to build Flaxmill Maltings.

[193] Pattison A., The *Darwins of Shrewsbury* (Stroud, 2009) p.74.

[194]This Mytton family appears in Shropshire briefly then disappears. https://www.british-history.ac.uk/vch/salop/vol10/pp368-380#p16 Accessed 24/02/2019.

[195] Information supplied by Muriel Lewis.

[196] http://www.shropshiresgreatoutdoors.co.uk/horse-riding/jack-mytton-way/ Accessed 31/03/2021

[197] http://www.madjacks.pub/jack-mytton-history-/jack-mytton-history.html# Accessed 18/11/2018 http://www.mytton.com/genealogy/pedigree.html

[198] https://shrewsburylocalhistory.org.uk/street-names/monkmoo. Accessed 20/08/2021.